THE
GOLDEN
GHETTO

8/1/00

To Jay –

Thank you so much for your insight & inspiration! I look forward to working with you in the future. Keep up the good work!

XO
Jessie

THE GOLDEN GHETTO

The Psychology of Affluence

JESSIE H. O'NEILL

WITH A FOREWORD BY
SHARON WEGSCHEIDER-CRUSE

 HAZELDEN®

Hazelden
Center City, Minnesota 55012-0176
1-800-328-0098 (Toll Free U.S., Canada, and the Virgin Islands)
1-612-257-4010 (Outside the U.S. and Canada)
1-612-257-1331 (24-hour FAX)
http://www.hazelden.org (World Wide Web site on Internet)

Library of Congress Cataloging-in-Publication Data
O'Neill, Jessie H., 1950–
    The golden ghetto : the psychology of affluence / Jessie H. O'Neill
    p.   cm.
    Includes bibliographical references and index.
    ISBN 1-56838-119-0
    1. O'Neill, Jessie H., 1950–   .   2. Spiritual biography—United States.
    3. Wealth—Psychological aspects.   4. Adult children of dysfunctional
    families.   5. Problem families—Psychological aspects.
    I. Title.
    BL73.044A3   1996   96–27220
    178—dc20   CIP
                02 01 00 99 98 97   9 8 7 6 5 4 3 2 1

Book design by Will H. Powers
Typesetting by Stanton Publication Services, Inc.
Cover design by David Spohn

Editor's note

Hazelden offers a variety of information on chemical dependency and related areas. Our publications do not necessarily represent Hazelden's programs, nor do they officially speak for any Twelve Step organization.

All the stories in this book are based on actual experiences. In some cases, the names and details have been changed to protect the privacy of the people involved.

The resources section contains information from *Taking Charge of Our Money, Our Values, and Our Lives: Guide to Forty Publications and Organizations.* © 1996 by Christopher Mogil and Anne Slepian for the Impact Project. All rights reserved. Reprinted with permission of the Impact Project.

This book is dedicated to all the courageous people who have so freely given their time and their stories to this endeavor. It is also dedicated to my mother, Rosemary Wilson Hoyle Austin, and my father, Joseph Philip Hoyle, for in spite of it all, they loved me more than anything in the world. But most of all this book is for my daughters, Rebecca and Maggie, in the hopes that by beginning to break the bonds of dysfunction, we can offer them a world in which the measure of a person's worth and the barometer of a person's happiness is not equated with the bottom line on his or her balance sheet.

CONTENTS

FOREWORD

Jessie H. O'Neill has written a book that is long overdue. In my twenty-five years as a family therapist, there were countless times I would have welcomed her book both for myself and for my clients.

In my work, I have encountered many wealthy families. I have been hired by the founder, patriarch, or matriarch often because they were having difficulty with children, in-laws, or grand-children. There seemed to be a great deal of concern about how the family heirs were going to handle the family business or fortune. Quite often, the heirs were unable or unwilling to live out the plans and wishes of the senior members of the family. This brought about anger, hurt, and estrangement. The heirs themselves felt inadequate, manipulated, and rebellious. There developed a breakdown in communication that necessitated help from an outside source. Fortunately, feelings could be expressed and ultimately healed when family members of all ages were willing to confront the issue of wealth directly.

Jessie's book addresses important topics such as addictions, workaholism, control, and narcissism and sheds light on the pain often involved in being wealthy—the unique variations on feelings of inadequacy, competition, jealousy. Working with trust fund young adults, I consistently found struggles with self-worth.

Too many felt ashamed of receiving handed-down wealth, guilty because they had so much, and inadequate when compared to the people in the family who made the fortune.

For years, the weight of the family fortune can sit on the shoulders of each generation, affecting people in ways they may not even recognize. I have seen children of wealthy families become alcoholic and the grandchildren respond in perfectionism and workaholism—which creates a family system that is a setup for new addiction. By the time three or four generations have passed, people are quite disconnected from the root cause of the problem which might very well have been the original wealth and the dynamics that were played out to achieve that wealth.

Both lay people and professional therapists will find this book most helpful in learning about the inner lives of the wealthy. Those from wealthy families will find the book most enlightening.

This book will help the reader find understanding, a sense of balance, and perhaps help him or her make peace with some of the issues of money.

SHARON WEGSCHEIDER-CRUSE
Author of *The Miracle of Recovery:*
Healing for Addicts, Adult Children & Co-Dependents
Consultant, Onsite Training
Family Therapist

PREFACE

When I went back to school at the age of forty for a master's degree in psychology and counseling, I was doing what I now would call "listening to my heart." This listening is something I constantly encourage my clients to do in their search for their own unique path. Before I, or my clients, can begin this journey in search of our hearts' messages, it is necessary to first heal our childhood wounds.

Over the years, as part of my own therapy and healing process, I had naturally begun to look at my family dynamics. This exercise was both painful and enlightening as I became aware that the presence of wealth had affected my family in countless ways, many of them negative. The dysfunctional relationship we all had with money seemed to directly contradict one of the driving myths of American life—that having money guarantees or is a prerequisite for happiness.

This realization led me on a search to learn more about the effects of wealth on individuals and on their relationships with others. This resulted for me in a "coming out" process wherein I finally began to own who I was and how growing up with wealth had affected me and my family. I spent months researching the topic only to discover that very little has been written about the damaging psychological effects of affluence. This book, to a large extent, breaks new ground.

As part of my research, I decided to interview wealthy people. But in order to discern whom I should interview, it was first necessary for me to define "affluence." This was, and still is, a difficult task. Realizing that each person's definition might be different, I quickly turned my search for a definition into an interview question. The responses I received were varied and interesting. A central theme wove affluence with a lack of "worry" about money—where it comes from and how we can pay for the things we "need." Peter Buffet, son of financier Warren Buffet, defined affluence simply as, "Having more than you need." Alex Forbes, a relative of Malcolm Forbes, suggested that "one [part] is an attitude that there is enough and that one need not get trapped in the hopelessness of there not being enough and that you have something to fall back on." She adds, however, that true affluence *should* mean that "you have either the inner resources or the outer resources to take care of your needs. There will be enough and you will find what you need. This is a sense of security that is not based on any amount of money."

For many wealthy people, as well as for those whose primary focus is the accumulation of money, it is precisely that inner security which is lacking. For our purposes here, I define an affluent person as someone who doesn't *have* to work in order to maintain a lifestyle that our culture would view as "upper class." In monetary terms, this definition would probably suggest a net worth of three million dollars or more, which would provide a substantial income independent of the principal.

The interviews with adults who grew up in affluent homes were the most interesting, difficult, and rewarding aspect of my research. I soon discovered that my experience of being raised in a family of affluence was not unique: The people I interviewed also reported many painful, often debilitating, and sometimes tragic experiences associated with growing up and living with wealth. Listening to their pain triggered my own. There was solace to be found, however, in the knowledge that I was no longer alone in this particular struggle. The mere acknowledgment of the problem—that, despite society's assumptions, wealth doesn't automatically provide happiness, that it often brings unhappiness, addiction, and feelings of inadequacy—was a powerful psychological release mechanism for those with whom I spoke.

* * * *

The road that has brought me to this work has been long and difficult, but always enlightening. My need to better understand myself has evolved into a desire to help others. I am now a psychotherapist in Milwaukee, Wisconsin, where I specialize in the treatment of adolescents and adults with wealth-related problems, codependency and addictions; many of my clients are "adult children" of dysfunctional homes (adults who were raised in dysfunctional family systems). I provide individual and group treatment as well as local and national workshops and seminars, using a combination of traditional and experiential therapy.

My professional training, as well as my personal experiences with alcoholism, food addiction, and Twelve Step programs, enable me to help those who are struggling with the addictive qualities of excessive buying, spending, gambling, and hoarding, all common behavioral dysfunctions of the wealthy. Through media coverage, both nationally and internationally, I have developed a growing clientele with whom I work primarily via long distance phone consultations, with only periodic face-to-face sessions.

I have discovered that as I accompany my clients on their journey to the heart, I grow and change in ways I never dreamed possible. My clients are my best teachers, and I know that I am most blessed to be where I am today, in the company of so many fine and courageous people.

Healing from the effects of growing up in the Golden Ghetto

has been a lifelong journey for me. Abundance has taken on a meaning that is less monetary and more spiritual. Over the last fifteen years, the once-terrifying freedom granted me by my inheritance has become a unique, gratifying, ever-changing gift. It has allowed me the time and resources to pursue those talents that support and nurture me on my physical, emotional, and spiritual journey to greater health and well-being. A great part of receiving and recognizing that gift has become the need to share the abundance I have been given. Each relationship that I form becomes healthier as I become healthier, and each day my life is filled with greater affluence, in the larger sense of the word.

Using the information at my disposal, I have tried to portray an honest picture of the benefits and problems of affluence. I have searched carefully for common threads between the professional literature and the personal interviews, and looked for similarities among the interview subjects. I will not pretend that my viewpoint is unbiased, for of course it is not. The vast majority of my hypotheses, as well as my firm conviction that the psychology of affluence is a topic worthy of attention, come from my own life experience.

ACKNOWLEDGMENTS

As is written in St. Luke 12:48, "To whom much is given, much is required." This book is an expression of my desire to extend my own healing and share my joy and gratitude through service to others.

I would like to thank my friend Bill Kauth, author of *A Circle of Men*, for all his support and networking that ultimately led to the publication of this book. Through him I was introduced to Mark Gerzon, author of *Coming into Our Own*. Mark in turn, sent this work on to his publisher, Jeremy Tarcher, who referred me to Joy Parker, whose unfailing editing, moral, and spiritual support have been a continual inspiration. The trail leads on to my agent, Sheryl B. Fullerton, whose faith and hard work led me and my manuscript into the friendly, accomplished, and professional hands of Steve Lehman, my editor at Hazelden Publishing. I feel privileged and blessed to have met and worked with people of such high integrity and commitment. I am deeply grateful to all of them for their generosity of spirit and their willingness to walk with me on this untraveled path.

INTRODUCTION

Growing Up in the Golden Ghetto

Money is the single most transformational substance in our society. It is seductive, alluring, fascinating, and perceived as greatly desirable. It is the American dream.

The positive effects of affluence are apparent, highly touted, and easily discernible. The goal of this book is to "balance the scale," to disclose the truth about the darker implications of acquiring and living with money. I hope to show how, upon closer examination, the American dream often reveals itself as anything but dreamlike. Dealing with the effects of affluence, more often than not, is difficult and debilitating. I contend that it is a rare and exceedingly well-balanced individual who can possess great material wealth and survive emotionally. It can be an intimidating and demanding task to create a stable, satisfying, happy life amidst the chaos of endless possibilities and choices.

For many years, I lived in the "Golden Ghetto." I was born into a family of affluence and later inherited much of that wealth—enough money to satisfy all of my material needs for life. Indeed, I was living the so-called American dream. Yet money was the prison that separated me from much of life: the consequences of my actions and attitudes, the larger reality of the world, and the possibility of fitting in with the other 98 percent of the population who inhabit that world.

My hypotheses on the psychology of affluence were born from my life experience of growing up in a wealthy dysfunctional home, and then reiterated in my research, interviews, and conversations with other affluent people. What I have found has been supported and consistently verified in my workshops, seminars, and private practice with wealthy and would-be wealthy clients.

One need not have a great deal of money to become entrapped by it. Today many Americans are working sixty, seventy, even eighty hours a week in an attempt to "make it" in today's corporate and professional worlds. The blue-collar worker, the unemployed, and the very poor who struggle to meet basic survival needs spend a great deal of their time and energy thinking about how to make money, and wishing they could make more. Their Golden Ghetto is only a fantasy, but it is no less destructive. No matter where we are on the ladder of financial aspirations, it never seems high enough. Rich and poor alike assume that more is always better. The specter of wealth, which our culture equates with happiness, is always out of reach, standing between us and whatever happiness life has already offered. The cost of maintaining this delusion can be the same for the nonwealthy as for the wealthy: it can cost them their families, their friends, and their souls.

This book is about healing our individual relationships with money and wealth. It reaches beyond the personal, however, offering suggestions about how we might undo the tremendous cultural damage that our beliefs about money, power, and happiness have inflicted upon us.

* * * *

My grandfather, Charles Erwin Wilson, was the founder of my family's original fortune, amassed during a long and illustrious career at General Motors. He gave up his considerable salary as president of General Motors to accept the position of secretary of defense under President Dwight D. Eisenhower. Though initially reluctant to do so, he considered it his duty to serve his president when asked. My mother, Rosemary Wilson Hoyle Austin, was next to the youngest of six children born to him and my grandmother, Jessie Curtis Wilson. My mother, after losing her first love in a fatal car accident, married my father, Joseph Philip Hoyle, at age seventeen. She was not willing to risk the loss of another love; ironically, my father told me that he was willing to marry prematurely because he was sure he would be killed in the war. Thus, they eloped, days before my father was shipped overseas to serve in World War II. Their honeymoon was a stolen weekend in my father's army barracks.

As was true of many young couples at that time, their decision, made in haste, was one that they would come to sorely regret. My father returned from the war five years later, and five long years after that I was born. They had tried everything they knew to conceive a child and had given up when my mother became pregnant with me. In spite of all that happened later in our family, I was wanted and loved from the very beginning.

I have no clear memories of my childhood. My earliest awareness of my parents' drinking problems stems from the time I was about eleven years old, although I believe they had both become alcoholics long before that, when I was still a very young child. In an era when martinis and Valium were a way of life among the affluent, they became hopelessly lost in a hazy world of booze, prescription drugs, and an aftermath of despair. Tragically, neither of them ever found their way to wellness.

As an adult seeking answers for my own distress and unhappiness, I discovered it is not unusual for the adult children of alcoholics to have gaps in their childhood memories. The size of the void depends on the level of dysfunction present in the household.

Sometimes I still feel that it is somehow my fault that I remember so little and that if I tried a little harder, I could recall much more—that maybe my childhood wasn't as bad as I think it was.

My mother died of a heart attack at age fifty-four, tired of fighting the cancer that repeatedly assaulted her body. It seems ironic that she died just as she was beginning to glimpse the possibility of a calmer, healthier, more spiritual life path. She had become very involved in church for the first time and was being exposed to new ways of looking at the world. I was twenty-eight when my mother died. I had recently separated from my first husband, was ensnared by my own alcoholism, and was bitterly angry at my parents for my unhappiness. My response to my mother's death was to increase my drinking and add cocaine to my arsenal of painkillers.

My father died while I was writing this book; he was seventy-eight. He spent his old age caught in the webs of alcoholism, denial of his declining health, reminiscence, and regrets. My response to my father's death was dramatically different from that of my mother's. I was forty-five, gratefully in recovery from my alcohol and drug addiction, and had my feet firmly upon my own life path as a mother, therapist, painter, and writer. I came home from the funeral to grieve the loss of a man I loved deeply; our relationship had been given the time and effort needed for healing and forgiveness.

I, like many affluent children, was raised primarily by surrogate caretakers: nannies, maids, and other servants. With a couple of exceptions, most of these caretakers had no emotional investment in their relationship with me, leaving me with memories that are decidedly one-sided (my side). In my therapeutic practice, I call these "one-dimensional memories." When combined with the psychological implications of growing up in a multi-dysfunctional home environment, these shadow memories of pseudo-bonding, a series of adult-child relationships nearly devoid of emotional content, become almost nonexistent. For years before I understood this dynamic, I struggled with what I called my "floating anxiety," a feeling that there was always something I needed to remember and something I needed to do. If only I could figure out what it was, I thought, then somehow everything would be all right. As a young adult, appearances were everything in my home. Looking good and impressing other wealthy people was much more important than the pursuit of self-knowledge. The popular media of the fifties and sixties painted the average American home in shades of "Ozzie and Harriet," and many baby boomers felt envy and shame because their homes in no way resembled that perfect world. I was no exception.

Not only did my childhood not resemble the popular sitcoms of the fifties, it didn't resemble any kind of normal household. Usually, chaos reigned supreme. My parents battled over anything and everything, stopping only to rest or to put on a face of reserved domestic harmony for the outside world. These engagements ran a level of intensity from petty bickering and casual, cruel asides to screaming matches and episodes of throwing things at one another. When my father was at work and my mother off on some social call or event and only the servants were present, a surreal calm overtook the days, a calm that only added to my confusion. The entire household, particularly my mother and I, was visibly more relaxed in the absence of my father's rage and venomous criticism. I vividly recall how the tension and fear would begin to build on a typical weekday as we silently waited for his return home. The staff would eagerly leave at five o'clock and my mother would begin to drink. As the alcohol loosened her emotional restraint, she frequently would direct her anger and bitterness at me or else spend hours on the phone complaining about my father to sympathetic friends — thereby excluding me completely. I quickly learned to prefer the latter option and, anticipating my mother's oncoming moods, would make myself scarce, stuffing down dinner as quickly as I could (I believe I ate 90 percent of my meals alone) and hurrying away to the fragile sanctity of my room.

Anxiety would form a knot in the pit of my stomach as I anticipated the slamming of the doors from the garage that signaled my father's return. He came home drunk more and more often as the years went by, and I learned to gauge the level of his intoxication by the way those doors closed behind him. When he hadn't come home by the time I went to bed, I was torn between relief and concern, and slept fitfully, still half listening for the sound of the doors and the inevitable battle between him and my mother. I remember countless nights of sleeping with a pillow over my head to block out the screaming. Which was real, the calm, sunny days or the screaming, drunken, terrifying nights?

My father's southern charm, good looks, and increasing financial success, backed by my mother's famous name and "old" money, ensured his popularity and acceptance anywhere he chose to go. With money no object, drinking, playing cards, and carousing with his buddies became increasingly more attractive than coming home to face the certain rage of my mother. Money made the escape from a failing marriage and the denial of his alcoholism infinitely easier.

As my father's addictive/compulsive behaviors increased, so did the enabling behaviors of his sister, my aunt Betty Hunt, who worked as his personal secretary and right-hand woman. Under her skilled care and guidance, my father's Cadillac dealership became more and more successful, allowing him to drink more and further cushioning him from the consequences of his destructive behaviors. Very few people are willing to "bite" or confront the hand that feeds them, and so my father surrounded himself with people who simply allowed—or worse, encouraged—his self-destruction. Friends or family who tried to intervene were simply avoided or met with rage and denial. In essence, because of the comfort and influence of his wealth, my father never hit the moral or physical bottom that frequently drives the addict to seek help.

In my mind's eye, I see my mother only briefly, framed momentarily in a doorway, as she hurries from room to room, fearful, preoccupied, and distant. She is always just out of my grasp. Her pain, confusion, and despair, expressed in frequent outbursts of anger and grief, are written plainly on her face. She makes little effort to hide her misery unless there are guests present.

Like all children of extremely dysfunctional families, I quickly developed a sixth sense, a hypervigilance that allowed me to instantly assess the level of potential conflict and abuse in any given circumstance and helped me survive emotionally within an often terrifying family system. My father's concept of child-rearing was a constant barrage of criticism, correction, humiliation, and intense verbal abuse. He could be bitterly sarcastic; when he was drunk, neither my mother nor I could do anything right. On the other hand, my mother's favorite strategy for molding my character was a facial and sometimes verbal expression of profound disappointment in me followed by emotional withdrawal. I blamed her distance on my inadequacies. As a young girl, I strove harder and harder to erase that perpetual look of sadness and disappointment from her eyes. However, as a young adult, I gave up and began to live up to her low expectations. After years of fighting my parents' message, unspoken and spoken, that I was not good enough, I finally internalized it and subconsciously set out to prove them right. Like many children of abusive, chaotic households, if I couldn't be "good" enough, I could certainly be "bad" enough.

I don't think too much of my father's anger was aimed at me when I was very young, but as I got older I joined my mother as the target of his dissatisfaction with life in general and with women in particular. I learned to foresee the level of danger that any given situation might hold and to use whatever means were at my disposal to avoid the confrontation. To this day, anger is the most difficult emotion for me to express in a healthy way and certainly still the most difficult for me to receive or observe. I know I am not alone in that fear. Many adult children of alcoholics are unable to express, deal with, or even feel anger. Because of an inordinate pressure on children of affluence to at least appear externally perfect, it is often particularly difficult for them to express any "unbecoming" emotion, especially anger.

The importance of this extreme emphasis on appearance in the affluent culture should not be dismissed. While it is true that ours is a culture, generally, in which enormous stress is placed on surface realities ("image is everything," as Andre Agassi puts it in the television commercial), appearance is even more grotesquely exigent in the subculture of wealth. As we shall see throughout this book, image often *is* almost everything in affluent society. There, behind the carefully constructed facades of material success, family order, personal power, and control, one often finds little in the way of ideas or behaviors that are not compromised by a preoccupation with externals and the pursuit of ego-gratification.

Holidays and vacations in my family were no respite from the emotional chaos. They seemed only to give both my parents an excuse to drink more and begin earlier in the day. The presence of servants, relatives, or friends sometimes softened the biting sarcasm that had become their favorite form of communication, but the presence of others also increased my fear that the embarrassing reality of our everyday lives would be discovered. My mother's perfectionism, driven, I believe, by her unlimited financial resources, made each social occasion an agonizing crescendo of disappointment, tears, and accusations of blame toward my father and me. We rarely managed to do whatever it was that we were supposed to do "right." Psychologically, I bounced from parent to parent, depending on who was simply available or the least disappointed, angry, or critical at the moment. I always failed either one or the other.

Between my parents, anger, resentment, and bitterness at a marriage turned sour ripened to hatred and rage as the years went by. At a time when people spoke the word *divorce* in subdued, judgmental whispers, I lived in constant fear that my parents were going to get one any day.

Assuming, as most children would, that my family's problems were somehow my fault, I began spending as much time away from home as possible and finally left for good when I was seventeen. I would visit for a few days on vacations from college and between summer jobs, always hoping that things had changed—and always being disappointed.

It is far beyond the ability of young children to know that it is not they who are wrong, but rather those towering, omnipotent adults whom they love so desperately and from whom they only want approval. Children begin as early as possible to use anything available to drown out the incessant, critical, heartbreaking messages from adults, all delivered "for our own good." At age four, as soon as I could reach the cookie jar, I began to nurture myself, calm the fear, and stuff the anger with food. To this day, I fight a daily battle with that oldest and most familiar enemy, compulsive eating.

I was an only child, and both my parents were emotionally unavailable, too distraught and addicted to alcohol and their own misery to provide even minimal support and reassurance. This is the story of too many children in our country, from all socio-economic backgrounds. But contrary to popular belief, money did not buffer the emotional devastation. Instead, it allowed my mother and my father to "buy out" of parenting, leaving me even further isolated emotionally—and often physically abandoned—in the "care" of a series of servants with little beyond a paycheck invested in our relationship. To most of them I was just their job. However, my first nanny, Gertrude, truly loved and cared for me from birth until age four. She left suddenly and without explanation one day, reinforcing very early for me the experience of abandonment by my parents. Children live in a small and egocentric world. They see themselves as the cause and recipient of everything that happens. They think, "I must have done something bad; I must *be* bad; I drove her away because I wasn't good enough." The seeds of shame are sown in childhood; I therefore blamed myself for Gertrude's disappearance. Shortly before my father died, I asked him why Gertrude had left us. I found out that she had simply been homesick and wanted to return to North Carolina and her own family. What had appeared to me as a child to be a devastating rejection and abandonment had a simple and reasonable explanation. The damage, however, was already done.

During adolescence, I desperately sought happiness and approval anywhere I could find it. I fluctuated frantically between overachievement and self-destruction, always walking a fine and dangerous line between the two. I met my first boyfriend at fourteen and was pregnant by the time I was sixteen. Terrified of how my parents might react, I tried to induce a miscarriage by jumping from roofs and bouncing down stairs. With nowhere else to go, I finally told my mother. We were on summer vacation in Walloon Lake, Michigan, and my boyfriend had left that morning to fly home to Florida. Concerned when I was unable to stop crying, she asked me what was wrong, and I told her. I will never forget the look of disbelief followed by pain and, finally, sympathy and pity.

Ashamed and afraid, I was unable to face my father; it was my mother who finally told him. Somehow the magnitude of my anguish broke through their ongoing misery and we pulled together as a family, perhaps for the only time. My father's abiding anger was briefly eclipsed by my obvious distress and suffering. He responded by arranging an illegal abortion for me. Buffered by drugs and the comforts of affluence, I awoke in our usual corner suite at the Plaza Hotel in New York City. There were no words of comfort, however, and none of recrimination. It was simply over. The family veneer of elite wealthy perfection was quickly reestablished, and our "shopping" trip to New York was never referred to again.

My abortion was buried so quickly and absolutely, with all the power and finesse money can buy, that twenty-five years passed before I was able to grieve the loss of the baby I never had. Back then, the experience only taught me an awful lesson: that I could get my parents' total attention by doing something "wrong" as well as, if not better than, by doing something "right." Shortly after the abortion, my boyfriend broke up with me with the words, "I hate fat, rich girls." Needless to say, his callous words inflicted a devastating blow on an adolescent's fledgling ability to trust men. More significantly, however, the word *rich* became linked to the shame I carried along with what was then only a few extra pounds. I recovered slowly, dazed and shocked—a changed person. My fist clenched, I was going to show the world: no one was ever going to get the best of me again.

Following that painful summer of 1966, I returned to Palm Beach Private for my senior year of high school. In a short time, I progressed from being a shy, overweight young woman to becoming the president of the student council, the lead in the senior play, and captain of one of the school's two athletic teams. I graduated with honors, receiving an award that acclaimed me the most accomplished all-around student. I had shed twenty pounds along the way, beginning my lifelong ride on the weight-loss merry-go-round. When rumors of my abortion began to circulate via a betrayed confidence, I lied and vehemently denied the truth—as I had been taught to do—further adding to the shame I carried. It is only in the past fifteen years, with the birth of my children and the loving support of friends, that I have begun to find parts of that abandoned, ashamed young woman. She was so obviously unlovable that even I had left her behind.

It is hardly surprising that shortly after my graduation from high school, I began drinking. On a graduation sailing trip to the

Bahamas, I got drunk for the first time. Not realizing that one of the signs of an alcoholic is the ability to consume large quantities of liquor with apparent impunity, I remember tending to others for hours as they became drunk and sick. I was one of the last to succumb, but spent the rest of the night leaning over the side of my bed vomiting onto the floor. It wasn't until the following fall at Rollins College that the memory of that first hangover faded enough for me to begin drinking in earnest. That abuse continued to escalate for fourteen years, culminating in my first Alcoholics Anonymous meeting in August 1981. This meeting was my first step in terms of personal spiritual growth and change, and it marked the beginning of my journey toward recovery.

During my two years at Rollins, I walked the tightrope between achievement and abuse that was to mark the next decade of my life. Pledging the "best" sorority on campus and becoming pinned to a boy from the "right" fraternity afforded me the external approval that I desperately sought. To what extent my family's money facilitated that process is uncertain; certainly it was an aid in some manner. I drank exotic and deadly punches made from grain alcohol and crawled into the dorm moments before curfew. At the time, it never occurred to me that the remedies I used to cure my loneliness, quell my shyness, and ensure my popularity were the beginnings of addictions I would have to battle later in life.

In retrospect, I know that alcohol enabled me to avoid facing my fear that no matter how fast I danced, no matter what I owned or where I lived, no matter whom I "loved" or who "loved" me, I still awoke the next morning alone with myself. Because of my emotionally vacant childhood and adolescence, the self that confronted me had no recognizable face or identity. I still believed with all my heart, however, that something outside of myself could make me happy. That, after all, is the overriding message of affluent culture: money, possessions, the right friends, the right experiences—happiness is only a matter of putting the external pieces together properly. When one remedy failed, I quickly added another or changed the script completely.

At the end of my freshman year, as suddenly as I had donned the preppie Villager skirts and Pappagallo shoes, I shed them for bell-bottomed blue jeans, bare feet, rings on my fingers, and bells on my toes. I ran away from Rollins College, my parents, and everything they stood for and spent the summer of 1968 in Haight-Ashbury. I joined the throngs of teenagers celebrating on Hippie Hill in Golden Gate Park, preaching "love, peace, and happiness." I played the guitar and sang my way through San Francisco during the Summer of Love, with its promise of "free" love and "free" drugs. But the love went sour and one day a stoned, laughing madman pulled a knife and held it to my throat as my fellow hippies stood frozen and watched. Depression and disillusionment began to nip at my heels again, the challenge and novelty of learning beckoned, and I returned to college that fall.

For me, however, the pendulum had swung from the Pi Beta Phi Sorority Pledge of the Year to token sorority hippie. My sophomore year I won the all-school creative writing award for my stories of San Francisco. This and the advice of a supportive and encouraging English professor inspired me to seek more fertile ground for my blossoming talent, and at the end of the year I left the lazy ways of Rollins. I transferred to the University of North Carolina at Chapel Hill where, challenged and stimulated, I graduated Phi Beta Kappa in the spring of 1971. It was here that I developed a love for writing and learning that has been the foundation upon which I have slowly rebuilt my shattered self-esteem. My college days at Chapel Hill were not unhappy. I managed, somewhat precariously, to balance my academic world and social life. I was popular, a "party girl," willing to do and try anything. Although the chaos whirled around me, the void within me seemed filled for a while. Anyway, I was accustomed to chaos.

My twenties, however, were a steady downhill slide. My parents went through a nasty divorce into which they selfishly and thoughtlessly dragged me, each courting me to take their side. Both threatened to subpoena me to testify in their behalf until, in outraged disbelief, I angrily told them I would not show up for either. Listening to endless distorted, angry tales of the pain and injury they received at each other's hands, I felt ashamed and embarrassed that they would share the intimate details of their failed marriage with me. As a result, I further withdrew emotionally from both of them.

My mother ran away with the captain of our yacht, a message delivered gleefully to me by a gossipy pseudo-friend of the family. My father's pride was mortally wounded: Mother had left him for an ex-navy man with a sixth-grade education, an employee, a man whom he had hired and paid for several years. In the world of the moneyed class, my mother could not have chosen a more painful way to "get even" with my father for all the years of neglect and misery. A man in awe of and controlled by wealth, my father felt betrayed not only by his wife, but by the money itself. In essence, he had paid another man to have an affair with his wife! Confusion and humiliation mingled with disbelief as my father watched my mother take up with someone he considered his inferior in every way. Like many in our culture, my father equated success with the amount of money a man earned. He could never understand or get over the fact that my mother chose such an "unsuccessful" man over him. Consumed with anger and hatred, my father increased his drinking. He never recovered from his bitterness, resentment, and rage. It slowly ate away at him, pushing him further down the road of alcoholism, depression, and self-destruction.

Not surprisingly, money became a primary focus in my parents' divorce. Accustomed to financial control and the ability to buy their way out of difficult situations, my parents battled ruthlessly. Money was both the weapon they wielded and the prize to be won. They argued bitterly and at great length, neither of them ever satisfied with the final settlement. As is true with many divorces of the affluent, the lawyers were the only winners.

After nearly a year of estrangement brought on by my anger and confusion about the divorce, my mother and I attained an uneasy reconciliation. Shortly thereafter, I "gave her away" at her second wedding to "that God-damned boat driver," as my father called him. My relationship with my mother, however, was never healthy or whole; it was volatile, conflicted, and filled with disappointment and hurt on both sides until her death.

I was twenty-one when I began to receive the income from a trust set up for me by my grandfather Wilson. Although it was not a huge amount of money, it allowed me the luxury of not having to work, at least not full-time. In an ironic reversal of my childhood, this money now allowed me to "buy out" of financial dependency on my parents. A minimal amount of contact with them had been necessary when I needed financial help during my college years; this was eliminated when the trust began to pay out. Months would pass without so much as a phone call between us. I was fairly young and an active alcoholic when my mother died, and it is as though I never knew her. I miss her to this day and have many regrets, the most painful being that she never got to see or hold her two beautiful granddaughters.

My father continued to drink until his death. Nonetheless, we attained a loving and forgiving truce several years before he died. It broke my heart to see him killing himself. In his own way he tried to reach out to me, and I know now that he did the best job he knew how to do. In later years he often spoke of his regret over "allowing" my mother to spoil me. Since he came from a more humble background than my mother, he was aware of the damage that was caused when she and the servants submitted to my every whim, and he periodically tried to intervene. According to him, my mother was adamant in her determination to give me all the things that she'd grown up with, and the intensity of her obsession was compounded by the fact that I was an only child. Following the unspoken power dynamics of money, my mother had the final say by virtue of her greater wealth.

Like many "good" daughters of alcoholic parents, my first marriage, at twenty-five, echoed theirs. Rhodes Berdan Baker, the eldest son of a wealthy Toledo, Ohio, family, and I had a short, party- and alcohol-filled, fight-ridden marriage that ended painfully but with little rancor. Still desperate for someone to love me, unable to be alone with myself, and with my biological clock ticking louder and louder, I jumped rapidly into a second marriage with the father of my children, Kevin Edgeworth O'Neill, in 1979. I was twenty-nine. Shortly after the birth of my first daughter, Rebecca, in 1980, I quit drinking with the help of AA and therapy and began my journey of recovery. My second daughter, Maggie, was born in 1983. In spite of my continuing sobriety, Kevin and I separated a few years later, our marriage of eight years ending for a myriad of reasons. However, my wealth did not play into our "irreconcilable differences." Because of Kevin's status as an attorney, he was not intimidated by my money, and it did not seem to affect the balance of power between us.

The last fifteen years have been filled with the joy of seeing the world more clearly each day. With two steps forward and one step backward I have slowly, and sometimes with great difficulty, acknowledged and forgiven my parents and myself for my past.

For some time now my past and present have been filled with my own recovery and healing process, raising my children, painting watercolors, writing this book, and further refining and defining my clinical work with people concerned with the dysfunctional psychological effects of money on themselves and their loved ones. I call these collective addictions, character flaws, psychological wounds, neuroses, and behavioral disorders caused or greatly exacerbated by the presence of or desire for excess money "affluenza." Culturally, affluenza manifests as a constipation or backup of the flow of money in our society. In individuals, it takes the form of a dysfunctional or unhealthy relationship with money and may manifest as shame, guilt, anger, rampant materialism, hoarding and/or all manner of addictive/compulsive behaviors.

In attempting to illuminate the negative psychological implications of possessing or pursuing great fortune, I am by no means unaware of the tremendously positive influence money plays in my daily existence. The awful, free-falling lack of control I experienced during my first thirty years has become a colorful vista filled with many possibilities—joyous choices yet to be made. I no longer approach each day with trepidation, but look forward to my life with anticipation and excitement. I am (finally) truly grateful for my affluence, in all ways.

I believe that those who are rich of spirit *and* rich in a monetary sense are in a unique and powerful position to literally help save the world. But to do so, to help save the world or even just ourselves, we, the wealthy, must learn to give fully of ourselves *and* our money, rather than hiding fearfully behind the barricaded walls of our "Golden Ghetto." It is time for the affluent to step forward with faith, confidence, and trust that the gifts we have received can be the means of connecting us with, not separating us from, *all* who comprise the world community.

1

MONEY IS AS MONEY DOES

Money brings some happiness. But after a certain point, it just brings more money.

NEIL SIMON

Money was meant to be our servant. But when we depend on servants too much they gradually become our masters, because we have surrendered to them our ability to run our own lives.

PHILIP SLATER
Wealth Addiction

LOUIS JORDAN ONCE DESCRIBED BEING IN A PLAY with a long run as living in a cage with gold bars—getting what we think we want can sometimes be more limiting than liberating. Living in a world defined by wealth can create a similar effect. While providing the means for solving certain life problems, money can create other, new problems that are by and large unique to the rich. For the nonwealthy, such problems seem to be a non-issue. If money truly created as much trouble as it helped alleviate, why would we be trying so hard all the time to get more and more of it? We all believe that making a lot of money is among the highest aspirations in this culture, or at least we behave as if we believe that; either way, the results are the same. The assumption is that we all want to increase our net worth and raise our standard of living and sense of safety and security in the world.

Nonwealthy people do not really care to hear about the troubles of the rich, whether those problems are genuine or not. When wealthy people talk about feelings of loneliness, alienation, or depression, they are usually greeted with responses such as, "Yeah, well, I'd love to have your problems," or, "You've sure got it rough, all right—I wish my life was so hard!" If you are among the vast majority in this country who consider themselves middle-class or below, you're probably thinking the same thing right now. The rich have "got it all." What more could they possibly want? What *are* they whining about?

The "Ghettoization" of the Monied Class

The purpose of this book is not to convince anyone to pity the rich. Pity is usually a demeaning emotion no matter at whom it is directed. It assumes the person being pitied lacks either free will or the capacity for self-directed thought and, therefore, the ability to grow and change. There is, therefore, no reason why anyone should pity anyone else solely on the basis of economic condition.

What I do hope to achieve here is an honest and forthright look at the psychological implications inherent in the pursuit or possession of wealth. My wish is that the information in this book will ultimately lead to better understanding, healing, and perhaps, even empathy between the wealthy and the nonwealthy. While pity separates us, empathy is an emotional state that brings us together, and it's my belief that our only hope of survival as a species is to increase a sense of our inter-relatedness, and decrease isolation and the internecine conflict it breeds. In other words, to increase the love and decrease the fear.

It is precisely the issue of isolation that leads me to define the subculture of wealth as a "golden ghetto." A ghetto is, after all, a place or condition in which a select group of people is separated from the majority. The majority often feels antipathy and discrimination, combined with fear and discomfort, toward the minority. These feelings fuel the separation between the haves and the have-nots. We fear that which we can't comprehend. If we have not experienced a feeling or situation first-hand, it is difficult to understand. I do not presume to insinuate that the golden ghettos of the rich are the same as the ghettos of poverty. There are vast and tragic differences that are a result of the lack of the basic necessities of survival in the ghettos of our poor. However, focusing on the differences, of which we are all too aware, will only drive us further apart.

Ghettos are created by internal psychological forces as well as external cultural forces. They are a symptom of an ailing society and a failure of our culture to support and nurture one another. Regardless of the origin of the ghetto, it works to wall off one particular subgroup, either metaphorically or literally. We usually assume that living in a ghetto is always in some sense involuntary, that ghettoization means one is somehow restricted from moving freely about in the culture as a whole by various combinations of the forces mentioned above. That is not necessarily the case.

If I say that the rich are culturally isolated from the non-rich in this country, I am unlikely to be contradicted. To contend, however, that this isolation is not necessarily either conscious or voluntary on their part, or even always desirable, may elicit some protest. This is a result of some of our common assumptions about the nature and potential of having excess wealth: (1) becoming rich and moving into the subculture of wealth are de facto positive and universal aspirations, (2) having money means having total freedom, (3) money fixes everything, and (4) the things that money can accomplish in one's life are precisely the things that hold the key to fulfillment, satisfaction, and psychological health — that is, money *can* buy happiness. This book will demonstrate why all of these assumptions are wrong by exploring the psychological implications of living in or aspiring to live in the subculture of wealth. It will examine the damage a culture-wide dysfunctional relationship with wealth wreaks on the rich, the non-rich, and our society. Then this book will look at strategies for healing the damage done to individuals as a first step toward healing our society. Suffice it to say here that the subculture of wealth can be seen as a ghetto phenomenon by virtue of certain key characteristics: there is ample evidence of physical, social, and cultural segregation; discrimination between the classes (imposed in both directions) plays a role in perpetuating this segregation; dual allegiances develop, with loyalty to the mores and practices of the wealthy often superseding those of the majority culture; cultural practices and assumptions exist that serve to defend the ghetto way of life against the impositions of the majority culture; and there is strong evidence of significant psychological and physical alienation from the majority culture.

Ghetto Life

A variety of social characteristics appear to evolve in a ghetto culture. Some are positive. Subgroups may choose to establish certain boundaries to protect themselves from the corruption and control of the dominant culture, as in the case of the Amish in this country. This may be the only way a subculture can maintain its integrity. This is mainly true for consciously formed and directed ghetto subgroups. On the other hand, such isolation, far from preserving the subgroup, may prevent a healthy and revitalizing cross-fertilization of ideas from the majority without which the ghetto degenerates over time, due to what could be described as psychological inbreeding. One result of this is the potential in ghetto culture for tradition and ritual to lose meaning over time by becoming rigidly dogmatic and preoccupied with external form.

Some individuals and subgroups respond to the limitations imposed by isolation by producing intense bursts of creative activity (the Harlem Renaissance, for example), but ghettoization can create exactly the opposite reaction as well. Cultural isolation can severely limit the range of possibilities in ghettos by circumscribing the groups' worldview, and thereby blunting creative imagination. The result may be a deep-seated belief that this is how it's always been; this is how it always will be. This belief may be arrogant or defeatist, but the end result—stagnation, disempowerment, hopelessness—is the same either way. To some extent, the golden ghetto contains each of the negative attributes of ghetto life listed above.

Who Owns Whom?

"So what?" you may very well ask. "So what if the rich live in a ghetto? It's a ghetto of luxury and leisure. It's a ghetto of seemingly endless choices. Isn't that what we all want? If they don't like it, why don't they just leave?" The rich certainly have the freedom to make those choices, a freedom accorded them by the money itself and therefore denied to the rest of us, we believe.

These questions are certainly understandable and, for the most part, quite reasonable. The answers, on the other hand, are often complex and difficult to grasp, especially for the nonwealthy. It is the purpose of this book, in part, to try to answer them. For now, let us simply say that, in the world of money, everything isn't always as it seems.

There is a saying in some farming communities that you don't own dairy cattle, they own you. If you've never had to get up at 4:30 in the morning every day, seven days a week, fifty-two weeks a year, to do the milking, you may not be able to fully appreciate the statement. Much the same can be said about wealth. The more money and possessions one has, the more time and energy one must invest in managing them. You may wish you had that problem right now. You probably think that you would really rather spend your time monitoring your assets and toys. Even if you enjoy your job and find a measure of fulfillment there, you would probably give it up for the job of attending to your money. We tend to assume that money only gives; we fail to see that it also takes, and the greater the wealth, the more it takes. Everyone would like to have a successful dairy farm, so to speak. But not everyone is willing to get up at 4:30 in the morning to ensure that success. For many of us, the price of money is too high to pay.

One way money takes, one way it controls us rather than the other way around, is to distract us from other, more important aspects of life. In *The Soul of Economies*, Denise Breton and Christopher Largent recount how Hindu philosophy describes four stages of human life. They are "student, householder, thinker (forest contemplative), and teacher (wandering monk)." Breton and Largent state that "moneymaking goes in the second: managing the household. But as important as it is, money isn't the pinnacle of human evolution. To treat it as if it were gets in the way of the larger development. We don't go beyond being householders."[1]

That is to say, we get sidetracked. We begin to think that money is all there is to life, or that all there is to life comes from money, which is just as irrational. We begin, as Philip Slater puts it in *Wealth Addiction*, "gradually to believe that money is the key to the satisfaction of all needs. At that point, money ceases to be a tool and becomes our master. It distracts our attention from those desires that money can't satisfy and directs it toward those it does. For if we have money we tend to think of what it can buy—we forget about our own needs and goals and become shoppers and catalogue readers."[2] In this sense, excess money doesn't free us, it imprisons us. It does this because we forget what money really is.

The Purpose of Money

Slater points out that money is a symbol, not a reality in and of itself. It functions as a tool in society, a means for homogenizing the value between disparate commodities—but money is not a result or end unto itself. When we assign value to the symbol itself, we get off track. Like the Hindu example given earlier, we focus exclusively on a fraction of what there is to experience and attend to in the world, only those aspects that can be homogenized, or given relative value for the purpose of exchange. What does that exclude? The majority of what I would call life: meaning, love, friendship, beauty, peace of mind, joy, a sense of place and purpose in the universe, and a connection to our spiritual selves. Focusing exclusively on the household part of life, ignoring the learning, thinking, teaching parts, we deny the existence of all values that cannot be bought or sold. When we do this, all the money in the world can't make up for the impoverishment we have created for ourselves.[3]

One of the reasons why we do this is that we believe in the principle of scarcity. We believe, as nineteenth-century economists Thomas Malthus and David Ricardo did, that the earth is limited and therefore so are its resources. In addition, we accept their assumption that humans have unlimited desires. The hypothesis they created from these observations is that there just isn't enough to go around, so we'd better grab what we can when we can and hold on to it. This is a fundamental premise behind just about any economic system, no matter how different they may seem on the surface. As Breton and Largent point out, however, "assuming that scarcity of resources limits economies is like assuming that chemical elements limit chemistry, food limits cooking, or notes limit music. The key lies not in what we have but what we do with it." We have neglected the management aspect of our resources and the creative intelligence that we use to make sense of them, to use them wisely and efficiently. We need to change our thinking about money. We need to understand that "economies don't exist for the purpose of driving up prices or garnering profits. They exist to serve the needs of humanity."[4]

The Bottom Line: The Suspension of Belief

Because we have individually and culturally pinned all our hopes on the promise that money buys happiness, we refuse to listen to anyone who might dare insinuate otherwise. Not only do we refuse, we fight it with immense anger, determination, and vehemence. It would amount to mutiny within our own homes and communities for many of us to begin to question the desirability of life in the golden ghetto. If that has been our hope, our dream, and our lifelong goal, then raising such questions could be the biggest challenge, with what appears to be the most risk, that we will ever undertake. I do not underestimate the immensity of the task. It requires great openness and willingness; it requires a suspension of beliefs.

It is not the acquisition or possession of wealth that is detrimental to our society. It is the intent behind it, the unconscious and blind attraction to life in the golden ghetto. Wealth is like intelligence—it is nice to have, but it doesn't mean your problems are over. It's how you use it.

Addiction to Money

In a sense, money is also like energy, or a catalytic substance that can create change by its mere presence. As such, money can be addictive, very much like alcohol and drugs are addictive. For the money addict, there is no such thing as enough money in the same way that there is no such thing as enough heroin for the smack junkie or enough booze for the alcoholic. One can be satiated temporarily by an addictive agent, but once you are hooked, there is no limit to the craving. Barring recovery (a form of remission) or death, the addict's need for the addictive substance or experience is infinite and forever. As an example, Slater points out that "a number of rich men have acknowledged that they could satisfy all their material needs—and even whims—with a fraction of what they hold, yet they are unable to stop trying to make more. Once money is given priority, there is no longer any basis for deciding when and where to stop accumulating." Money addicts like Texas oil billionaire H. L. Hunt will continually confuse means and ends. They know how to produce the tools; they just haven't any idea what the task is that the tools are for. "H. L. Hunt, once thought to be the richest man alive, was quoted as saying, 'Money is nothing. It's something to make the bookkeeping convenient.' Yet he devoted his life to the accumulation of this 'nothing,'" writes Slater. Henry Ford and Hunt and other rich men may have lived simply and without ostentation, he observes, but "if money was of no interest to them, why did they amass so much of it? Why didn't they give it away? Who keeps old scorecards? H. L. Hunt may have lived simply, but he was notorious in refusing to give the money he didn't care for to charitable causes. When wealth addicts say they're not interested in money, what they usually mean is that they're not interested in spending it."[5]

It is not uncommon for the wealthiest people in our country to have the greatest difficulty in giving their money away, even to charitable causes. Only 20 percent of rich people make charitable bequests. Households earning in excess of $100,000 a year give a lower percentage of their income (2.5 percent) than those who earn $10,000 a year or less (3.6 percent). In addition, estimates are that the lifetime giving of the more than 2,500 households in America with a net worth exceeding $100 million totals less than one-half of 1 percent of net worth.[6] As mentioned earlier, this results in a back-up of the flow of money in our society.

Slater's signs of wealth addiction include the type of obsessive parsimony described above, as well as the confusion of ends and means mentioned earlier. He also includes a tendency to greater ownership of material things with a corresponding decrease in actually using them. His fourth symptom of wealth addiction is restlessness and chronic search behavior. This symptom may afflict rich or poor and is characterized by an endless quest for more without consideration of the long-term consequences. Wealth addicts searching for more "are the kind of people," writes Slater, "who build nuclear power plants *before* figuring out how to dispose of the atomic wastes."[7]

Wealth Addicts Are Made, Not Born

The greater part of this book is devoted to exploring the psychological results of dysfunctional relationships with money. For example, consider here one scenario that is commonly played out in the homes of the rich across our nation. A wealthy child, isolated and overprotected from the world that he or she will eventually be called on to live in and support, fails to develop the subtle nuances of understanding and strength of character required to successfully navigate the larger social milieu. This lack of socialization combined with society's condemnation and expectations ultimately weakens rather than strengthens the person's ego and personality structure.

Children want to be a part of the world that they see when they look around them. They want to know their place in it. When they are prevented from participating in this world because it is too dangerous, not good enough, or peopled by the "wrong" types, a few things happen. First of all, they feel different from others. Few of us can bear to feel different for long without developing a need to give ourselves reasons for why we feel different. The children of wealth may adopt their parents' reasons for this feeling, perhaps concluding that others are not their equals, or that other people won't understand their special ways of behaving or thinking, or that others will be envious and want to possess what they possess. Rather than make the child more self-confident, however, this increases his or her fear of the world. The child feels isolated, as if he or she doesn't belong. Children who are held back from participation in everyday life tend to develop one-dimensional social skills that are excellent within the wealthy society, but inept, unskilled, and uncomfortable outside of it. They tend to insulate themselves from the world, and the cycle starts anew with the next generation.

People who grow up in the golden ghetto often feel isolated and marginalized in society at large. Though they may be at the top of the heap, they don't fully know or understand what or who it is that is under them. In a country like America, where hard work is valued and the majority rules, people who grow up with wealth can feel deeply conflicted about their position in respect to other people. They may feel guilt at having it easier than others, or fear of how they are viewed by the nonwealthy. They may also feel like frauds. Let's face it, we are seldom all that we appear to be, and the more glittering and attractive the external package, the greater the inner sense of dishonesty a person might feel for not living up to a larger-than-life image.

The Need for Healing

Much more could be written about the philosophy of money and economies, but that is beyond the scope of this book. Our focus here is on the lives of those who inhabit the golden ghetto, the forces and psychological traumas that drive them into dysfunctional, unhappy lives, and the possibility of treating their affluenza so they can leave their ghetto and rejoin the world.

The truth is, we who have so much can't afford to hide fearfully in our golden ghettos any longer. The wealthy control the majority of the earth's natural and financial resources, and we have made a mess of things. Greed and denial prevail over wise use and altruism. We shove our heads deeper and deeper into the sand with the hope that no one will see us, with the hope that someone else will clean up the mess we have made, with the desperate hope that if we look the other way long enough, things will get better. In reality, all the gold in the world can't buy us peace as long as we live separately from each other, from the world, and from our true selves.

Money is powerful and transformational, but money has no intrinsic spiritual value. For money to have meaning, we have to control it, creating the context within which it becomes a spiritual entity. It will do what we demand of it, but we must be strong enough and focused enough to know what it is that we want it to do. Left to its own devices, it controls us. Our lives speed by in a flurry of financial caretaking, time-consuming "responsibilities" that allow no opportunities for listening to our hearts or the cries of those around us.

The unprecedented affluence that followed World War II has

lulled us as a nation into a false sense of entitlement much as it lulls an individual who inherits money. We somehow think that we not only deserve wealth, but that it is our right. We pout and sulk when it does not appear. One only need look back in history to realize what a preposterous and damaging assumption that is. What we have failed to do is to use our affluence for the benefit of the earth and humankind. As a culture, we have been on a mindless, selfish binge to see how much money we can individually accumulate. Material wealth became the earmark of success, the way we kept score; but one day when we weren't paying attention, we became addicted to it. If this much feels good, we told ourselves, then more would feel better.

Somewhere, many years ago, we lost ourselves in the process. Money was originally invented to barter for the essentials of survival. But then the money itself became the primary goal and the essentials became secondary. We have lost track of what money is for, and it is time to do a cultural intervention on our abuse of money. We must begin to make conscious choices about the disposition of our wealth before we no longer have the luxury of making any choices at all.

Because there is currently such a vast chasm in our world between the haves and the have-nots, we have perhaps naively assumed that what is missing is more money—that if only the poor became rich, then everything would sort itself out. What we have failed to realize is that we don't need more wealth; we need to use what we have differently. But before anyone is going to be willing to do that, we have to understand the nature of the beast. Hating and resenting the rich because they have more than you do is downright counterproductive in terms of eliciting change. No one and nothing changes through hatred. People change when they feel safe enough to look at the darkness within. They change when they feel supported and nurtured. People change slowly and gently with love from within and without. If you must be angry, be angry with the dysfunctions of affluenza, not with the individuals, perhaps including yourself, who have been unthinkingly trapped in the illusion of the American dream. Make a decision to change individually and to use your resources—financial, intellectual, and spiritual—to make a difference within the cultural institutions that continue to perpetuate the lies about wealth and money.

In this book, I hope to portray an accurate picture of those who live in and around the golden ghetto. I will examine their unique issues and problems, how some of them cope, for better or for worse, and offer suggestions to those who still struggle with money-related issues. I will take a further look at affluenza, what it is, and how it has become a cultural malaise. In so doing, it is my deepest hope that the abyss which separates the affluent from their fellow travelers, an abyss created by false boundaries and the myth of the American dream, will begin to disappear. Collectively, we *can* heal our society, but we must begin by healing ourselves.

NOTES

1. Denise Breton and Christopher Largent, *The Soul of Economies: Spiritual Evolution Goes to the Marketplace* (Wilmington, D.E.: Idea House, 1991), 199.
2. Philip Slater, *Wealth Addiction* (New York: E.P. Dutton, 1980), 12–13.
3. Ibid. 3, 12–13.
4. Breton and Largent, *The Soul of Economies*, 33–34.
5. Slater, *Wealth Addiction*, 11, 35–36, 43.
6. "Lessons from Wingspread: A Report of Recommended Strategies for Promoting Philanthropy (Boston: Philanthropic Initiative), quoted in *More Than Money*, no. 9, (Autumn 1995): 9.
7. Slater, *Wealth Addiction*, 53–55.

2

AFFLUENZA:
THE DYSFUNCTIONS
OF MONEY

Wealth as a primary relationship shares some of the symptomatology of addiction to any substance though wealth, like a genie in a jar, is able to take on, almost magically, a vast variety of enticing forms and shapes. The persuasive and seductive dream of happiness that the acquisition of wealth carries with it indentures one to a lifelong devotion to the attainment of that goal postponing the real act of living until one's "ship comes in."

TIAN DAYTON
Trickle Down Wealthonomics or
The Falcon-Crest Syndrome

THE GOLDEN GHETTO IS INHABITED BY PEOPLE
from all walks of life who are bound together by a common illusion: the myth of the American dream, the conviction that money
can, does, and should guarantee happiness. Consequently, this is a
ghetto with no socioeconomic walls. It is as much about the fac-
tory worker who wastes his potential for happiness fantasizing
about being rich as it is about the wealthy person whose life is
void of meaningful relationships and filled with nothing but work
and the accumulation of money. It encompasses the middle-class
couple who both work two jobs and whose children spend the
majority of their waking hours in the care of strangers—not because they need the money to survive but because they believe
that the accumulation of more material possessions will bring
them happiness and fulfillment. The people who live in the
golden ghetto all suffer from affluenza.

As my story and the rest of this book will illustrate, our culture
holds many misconceptions about wealth, about those who have
it, and about those who spend their lives trying to accumulate it.
This chapter will discuss some of the psychological dynamics of
our relationships with money and unveil some of the myths that
surround it. The following six ideas lay the groundwork for understanding the psychology of affluence and for finding a way out
of the golden ghetto:

1. The psychological dysfunctions of affluence—"affluenza"—are generational and are often set in motion
   by the Family Founder.
2. Workaholism isolates the Family Founder as well as
   individual family members; absence of parents and
   turnover of reliable caretakers create abandonment
   and trust issues for the children of affluence that follow them into adulthood.
3. Inherited or sudden wealth can create a false sense

of entitlement, a loss of future motivation, and an inability to delay gratification and tolerate frustration.

4. Inheriting money can seriously damage self-esteem, self-worth, and self-confidence.

5. Society holds a highly ambivalent attitude toward the wealthy that often manifests as reverse snobbery, or "wealthism."[1]

6. The idea of the American dream, that the pursuit of money is among the highest of aspirations and that affluence is synonymous with happiness, is a persistent and pernicious cultural myth.

The psychological dysfunctions of affluence — "affluenza" — are generational and are often set in motion by the Family Founder.

Family Founders frequently suffer from addictive/compulsive behavior, often in the form of workaholism, which causes them to virtually abandon their families, physically and emotionally.

My grandfather C. E. Wilson's ascent up the corporate ladder to the presidency of General Motors, followed by his appointment as secretary of defense, was the quintessential American dream, "rags to riches" story. He worked long and hard and was often required to be absent from his family. After his retirement, he managed and traveled between four homes, two of which were working beef and dairy cattle operations. He discovered, as most Family Founders do, that maintaining one's accumulated wealth is itself a time-consuming and challenging task.

When I was nine or ten years old, I spent the summer at Teljer Lodge, my grandparent's summer home on Walloon Lake, Michigan. I remember my grandfather being there only a few days during the entire summer. My grandmother, Jessie, would hoist the flag when he was in residence and take it down when he left. It was a way of letting everyone on the lake know when he was home. I remember that he was a warm and gentle man who seemed to love us all very much, but I never got to know him very well; he died when I was only eleven. Although warned by doctors and family to slow down after his first minor heart attack, he continued living life at an extraordinarily fast pace, saying that he had always lived that way and had no intention of changing. Two years later, in 1961, he was dead.

What was regarded in his day as the good old-fashioned work ethic is now also recognized as one route to a type of compulsive behavior, workaholism—prevalent today throughout the economic strata of our society. Workaholism is a condition closely related to what some psychologists call "addiction to chaos," a driving need for frenetic activity as a means of avoiding feelings. People who are addicted to chaos tend to thrive on, and even manufacture, constant drama and upheaval in their personal and professional relationships. Although filled with apparent "feeling," this high drama does not touch the emotional core of the individual and is often a subconsciously directed strategy to avoid real intimacy.

The living nightmare of the addictive/compulsive personality is called cross-addiction. When one addiction, such as workaholism, has been successfully treated, it is not unusual for another to appear in its place. In addition, parents with compulsive or addictive tendencies often produce children with the same tendencies, although the specific type of addiction, or "drug of choice," might be different. For example, there is a high correlation between paternal alcoholism and daughters with eating disorders. The latter is an extension of the need to appear perfect and feel in control in an out-of-control, far-from-perfect home environment.

I believe that any particular type of addictive behavior results from a combination of genetic predisposition and a dysfunctional family system. It constitutes one part of an attempt to self-treat or cope with the "broken" or missing emotional, physical, and spiritual parts of the individual. The good news is that the cycle can be broken, but seldom without some sort of treatment or intervention. Though family dysfunctions are passed down through the generations, my own experience, and that of many of my clients, shows that if we choose effective methods of treatment, awareness, and change over compulsion or addiction, we can break the generational cycle.

Workaholism isolates the Family Founder as well as individual family members; absence of parents and turnover of reliable caretakers create abandonment and trust issues for the children of affluence that follow them into adulthood.

Affluence allows parents to "buy out" of parenting by turning the children over to the care of a series of surrogate caretakers. Raised in "splendid" isolation, these children are deprived of the socialization that takes place within the families or day-care facilities of their less-affluent counterparts. This is only one of the many ways in which children of affluence are set apart from their peers. Consequently, they often suffer from extreme feelings of loneliness and isolation.

With increased affluence and the progression of workaholism, Family Founders find it more and more difficult to trust others and form or sustain intimate relationships. Since "water seeks its own level," they frequently choose driven, narcissistic, externally preoccupied people to marry. The combined effects of affluence and an emotionally and physically distant parenting style create children who have low self-esteem and a highly difficult time trusting and forming lasting intimate relationships of their own. The children's lives are often then characterized by a series of broken marriages or unhappy, unsatisfactory relationships.

Although working excessively is still regarded by many as a "positive" addiction, in reality it greatly increases the risk that children will experience the parents' absence as a potentially devastating form of abandonment. A child is not able to process, either intellectually or emotionally, why a parent is not present and can only assume at some level that this absence is the child's own fault. She or he concludes: "My mother and father are not here. They don't love me. I must be unlovable." The crippling effects of absent parents cross every economic boundary. It is a startling fact that the same feelings of low self-esteem, self-blame, and lack of self-confidence are equally present in both children of affluence and children born into extreme poverty.[2] This subject will be more fully explored in chapter 4.

Money is seductive, alluring, fascinating, and perceived as generally desirable. When wealth is present in a relationship, it changes the course of that relationship in a number of different ways, depending upon whether the wealth is evenly distributed and shared, or held primarily by the man or woman. Most people perceive money and power as synonymous, which bestows on the possessor of the wealth the majority of the power in the relationship, frequently creating an unresolvable imbalance. At the very least, when there is great or increasing wealth present in a relationship, it becomes a primary focus that can distract the couple from the more difficult tasks of parenting, negotiating healthy boundaries, and sharing feelings. Again, as a result of the false assumption that money is inherently "good" and will automatically help a relationship, it can become an invisible and unrecognized barrier to intimacy.

In many subtle and not so subtle ways, the affluent are socialized from early childhood to assume that people are out to "get" their money. In a recent article in *Milwaukee Magazine,* a wealthy man who wished to remain anonymous is quoted, "And then . . . my mother was very particular about my bringing friends home. There was always this underlying theme . . . they aren't your real . . . 'equals.' So I never had any friends over."[3] Wealthy heirs are constantly warned never to discuss their financial status with anyone outside the family. They are taught that nonaffluents are not their equals, and discouraged from socializing with them through parental admonitions such as, "They're not one of us." Is it any wonder that they become isolated, lonely, and suspicious of their acquaintances?

These parental and class expectations are to a large degree responsible for an unhealthy air of secrecy that permeates the world of wealth. Upon hearing the subject of my book, my dinner partner at a fundraiser responded, "Well! We just don't talk about those things!" All of the wealthy individuals interviewed for the *Milwaukee Magazine* article quoted above chose to remain anonymous. This choice may loudly attest to a degree of shame underlying their feelings regarding the family fortune.

The barrier to intimacy that money creates works both ways, particularly for wealthy women attempting relationships with nonwealthy men. Many wealthy women find it nearly impossible to maintain a perceived "balance of power" in relationships with men who have less money. Since our culture has traditionally defined men as inherently more powerful than women, most men eventually become acutely distressed by an imbalance tilted in the opposite direction, toward women, as a result of a woman's greater wealth. One man with whom I was involved was always trying to "keep up" and pay his half even though I was comfortable paying for the majority of our entertainment and travel. Never, to my knowledge, did I in any instance use my money as a source of retribution or humiliation. Yet eventually, he came to the poignant and painful conclusion that my wealth so diminished what he had previously seen as an adequate and respectable income that he simply could not cope with what he perceived as the "unfairness" of it. His pride and ego were so closely tied to the amount of money he could contribute to the relationship that by having less than I, he felt as if he *were* less than I. We discussed this problem often and openly, acknowledging the destructive effects this belief had on our relationship, but to no avail. This perceived "inequity" was one of the main reasons the relationship ended painfully after five uneasy years, even though we still loved one another. As I have spoken to other wealthy women, I have discovered that my experience, unfortunately, is the rule rather than the exception. The psychological dynamics of money, gender, and power are further explored in chapter 5.

Sadly, some people genuinely care more for the money than for the person in a relationship. These people, too, in their inversion of values, are victims of their acceptance of the American dream. In their obsessive, unexamined attraction to money, they attempt to maneuver closer to the wealth, vaguely assuming they will somehow benefit from this proximity. Along with celebrities and the politically powerful, the wealthy learn, over the years, to recognize "wealth groupies" and keep their distance from them. This necessity to be constantly on guard against ingratiating flattery and insincere motives is another reason the affluent find it difficult to trust others.

Inherited or sudden wealth can create a false sense of entitlement, a loss of future motivation, and an inability to delay gratification and tolerate frustration.

Emotional deprivation and material satiation of children produce adolescents and adults who suffer from a false sense of entitlement, a high degree of neediness in their relationships, an inability to delay gratification and tolerate frustration, and loss of future motivation. Since addiction is believed to be partly genetic and generational, they often suffer from variations of the addictive/compulsive behaviors of their parents or the Family Founder.

The deference our culture grants to money and therefore to

the owners of it can elicit character traits and behaviors in the wealthy that are every bit as unattractive as those of the wealth groupie. When an affluent individual is continually treated as though he or she is somehow special and better than others, an expectation of deference builds over time which is the cornerstone of snobbish behavior. With the addition of a little denial and false pride, wealthy people can convince themselves that it is their superior character or personal destiny that draws others to them. Relationships formed under such assumptions can therefore be extremely ego-gratifying and satisfying for a time. Inevitably, however, the imbalance of power and the fact that the foundation for intimacy is based on mutual self-deception—illusions of money as a moral presence, false entitlement, and so on—leads to the erosion of the relationship's structure. The result is invariably resentment, envy, loss of trust, passive-aggressiveness, and other destructive feelings and behaviors.

Not only is false entitlement toxic to intimate relationships, but it can be socially noxious and divisive as well. An old friend of mine is dating a wealthy woman who often exhibits signs of an inflated sense of self-worth that, in my practice, usually indicates deep feelings of insecurity. When my friend Leonard and I ran into this couple in a restaurant a few weeks ago, Leonard asked her to remind him who she was. The woman looked at him incredulously, obviously unable to believe he couldn't remember. Surely everyone knew who *she* was and should instantly recognize her! She sputtered out her name in a condescending and contemptuous voice and then turned to her date in an obvious attempt to snub Leonard. As we left, I explained what had transpired to my friend, who found the situation amusing. It had all flown blithely over his head. It is often the people who are not impressed enough by money to remember a rich person's name who are best suited to engage in an honest friendship with a person of wealth. The presence of the money is less likely to engender a sense of inequality: suspicion of the other's motives on the one hand and feelings of envy or insecurity on the other.

Embarrassing accounts of the rich and famous demonstrating the inability to tolerate frustration or delay gratification abound in the media and our literature. To the disgust of the average-income person, who often waits long and patiently for the smallest reward, the affluent frequently demand instant and preferential treatment in restaurants, hotels, shops, and other public places. If, as children or young adults, these individuals were surrounded by obsequious servants, money groupies, or parents who granted their every whim, it is not surprising that they would expect the same treatment when they became adults. Fortunately, these unattractive and socially divisive behaviors and the beliefs underlying them respond extremely well to gentle, supportive therapeutic treatment.

Because of these offensive traits, however, many rich people alienate the individuals with whom they might have healthy relationships. Consequently, they may live lonely lives, surrounded by "hangers-on" who ignore their inappropriate behavior in order to gain access to their money. Receiving no honest, loving feedback, these affluent people become more and more alienated from themselves and others as they vainly attempt to fill their inner void with the various status opportunities that wealth affords. In addition, their wealth feeds the generational dysfunctions that they have also inherited from their parents.

These generational dysfunctions and genetic predispositions frequently take the form of addictive/compulsive behaviors: alcoholism, drug addiction, compulsive gambling and spending, and other behaviors involving the use of large sums of money. These inappropriate attempts to cope are also a function of the inheritor's inability to delay gratification and tolerate the everyday frustrations of life. This component of affluenza will be examined and explained in more detail in chapter 3.

Rich or poor, if individuals are comfortable with who *they* are, then they are more likely to be at ease with a person of wealth or power. Psychological health and security is not easily threatened by hollow external symbols of power.

Inheriting money can seriously damage self-esteem,
self-worth, and self-confidence.

Unlike Family Founders who develop high self-esteem by making the original fortune, those who inherit wealth often live their entire lives wondering if they could have made it on their own. In order to be considered "successful," they must surpass the accomplishments of the previous generation. To simply maintain the existing level of affluence is often perceived as failure by everyone concerned. Thus, another common symptom of affluenza is self-doubt and the persistent suspicion that all of one's accomplishments are invalid because the money made one's achievements easier.

It is part of our psychological makeup to deem things that are easy to attain as lacking in merit and worthy of little attention. When accomplishments come too easily, as they sometimes do to the rich, they are seldom judged by our society as real successes. Certainly, there is a clear measure of fairness in such an assessment. A typical cultural attitude toward the affluent is reflected in the words of former Texas Governor Ann Richards, who once said of former President George Bush, "He was born on third base and thinks he hit a triple." While this may or may not be true of Mr. Bush in particular, the act of struggling does give public and, frequently, personal credence and value to our accomplishments. Wealth shelters one from many of the challenging and difficult, yet character-building, tasks of life. This often leaves one weaker, however, and even less prepared for life's next onslaught. That which does not kill us makes us stronger — except when we buy our way out of it.

Our cultural assumption that money or wealth *always* makes life better and easier can be misleading, however. An article in *The New York Times Magazine* recounts the dilemma of William Post, who won $16.2 million in the Pennsylvania lottery. Within five years of this windfall, his life had fallen apart. His brother had been charged with trying to hire someone to murder Post and his wife (his sixth by that point in time) for their money. The article noted, "Post said he was more content before he won, when all he had was a job with the traveling circus cooking for the thin man and the lion tamer. Friends and family begged or borrowed from him; business ventures failed; an ex-girlfriend sued."[4]

Because of the tendency to dismiss the accomplishments of the rich, many people born into wealth compensate by choosing careers or avocations that are academically, artistically, or physically demanding. The perception is that excellence in these types of pursuits are more difficult to "buy" since success is more likely to depend on some mix of intelligence, talent, diligence, or physical prowess. Therefore, accomplishments in these areas will generally bolster self-esteem and a belief in one's own ability to succeed.

The truth is that there *are* enormous career advantages to being wealthy. It's easier to market yourself — *if* you first find the self-esteem and self-worth to believe you are marketable. You can pay for and receive advanced training or education — *if* you believe you are smart enough and worthy of such success. The extra funds give you the ability to endure the inevitable lack of financial success as you build a practice or career — *if* you have the ability to delay gratification and tolerate frustration, which many of the wealthy lack. The money can work to your advantage in many ways — *if* you have the strength of character that having wealth, particularly inherited money, often destroys.

Society holds a highly ambivalent attitude toward the wealthy that often manifests as reverse snobbery, or "wealthism."

Affluent people often encounter jealousy and envy from their less-affluent acquaintances. As we have seen, this prejudice against the rich may include a discounting of their accomplishments and abilities, and an uncritical assumption that they "bought" their success.

My fundamental theories about the negative effects of affluence on the individual, based upon my own experience and observations, have been supported and validated by my research. I have seen my own life mirrored in the few books and articles I found on the subject and have heard my personal story retold, with slight variation, by each wealthy person I interviewed. I've also found these observations reiterated in the case histories of my clients. What surprised me and provided me with new insights was how little is available in the professional literature on the psychological effects of money on the *individual.* There are rooms full of research on affluent societies: the effects that wealth, or the lack of it, has on cultures and countries as a whole.

What little information there is on the psychology of the affluent individual has usually been written by people who are not a part of what they assume to be a "privileged world." Although their observations are recorded sincerely and to the best of their abilities, they are invariably writing from the outside, looking in. Erroneous assumptions, faulty perceptions, and covert prejudices tend to run throughout these articles and books. The authors are often quick to assure the reader that they are *not* one of the people they write about. Sometimes the envy and resentment are overt in their expression of disdain for the "idle" rich. A tendency to discount accomplishments of the wealthy translates at times into an assumption that the negative effects of wealth are not as devastating as the rich themselves report.

The sum of these hostile viewpoints forms a type of prejudice termed "wealthism." In my opinion, these preconceptions and misconceptions vastly alter the perspective of these writers and their ability to report the true effects of wealth. One reason why many of my clients are willing to work with me by phone, rather than with a local therapist in person, is that they have frequently run into wealthism in their previous therapeutic relationships. At the very least, they found that psychotherapists who have not developed at least some version of the concept of affluenza were not able to understand their wealth-related problems. Two wealthy acquaintances are working separately with the same local therapist. I was not surprised when each independently confided that, when they shared their relationship difficulties with this counselor, his unsympathetic response was, "I just don't understand the problem. Aren't there enough (Kennedy, Rockefeller, etc.) boys to go around?" The painful details of their lives became, for him, a bad joke because of the popular notion that if you have money, you don't really have any problems.

It is not difficult to see why there is resentment, envy, anger, and hatred toward the rich when so many people are starving and homeless. Yet it also becomes difficult for some wealthy people to give of their time or their money as a result of a diffuse but growing animosity toward them along with the perceived threat of outright violence. The entire situation becomes a dangerous, culture-threatening catch-22: because of their fear, the wealthy retreat behind walled communities, further hoarding their resources and widening the cultural and economic divide.

How do we end this spiral of fear and resentment? Sometimes the easiest way out is not a straight line. Although the problems of poverty far outweigh the problems of affluence, we cannot solve the enormous social problems we are facing without the financial resources, skills, and knowledge of the rich. That is why the healing of the wealthy plays a vital part in healing our society.

If empathy and understanding can begin to grow where there has only been hatred and fear, we may yet find a way to save our country from financial and spiritual bankruptcy.

The idea of the American dream, that the pursuit of money is among the highest of aspirations and that affluence is synonymous with happiness, is a persistent and pernicious cultural myth.

Protected by the secrecy and mystery surrounding the subject of affluence, the myth of the American dream persists. People still believe that money buys happiness; it is a tenacious and erroneous conviction.

A book review in *The Wall Street Journal* of a recent biography of oil tycoon Jean Paul Getty sported the headline "Money Does Buy Happiness." The reviewer is dismissive of the role money played in the spectacular disintegration of the Getty family. He is "not sure the tragedies that occurred in the Getty family were not in this modern life statistically probable." The review seems to celebrate the observation that Getty pursued "affairs [as] his favorite means of exercise and relaxation. . . . He was a lousy father, ignoring his children, and a terrible husband . . . [whose] sole pleasure in life, apart from fornication, was making money. . . . He was a cheapskate of Scrooge-like dimensions, vengeful and snobbish." For the reviewer, who is himself apparently wealthy, this is scant evidence of dysfunction. He shrugs off the suicide, multiple divorces, and drug and alcohol addiction of some of the Getty children as just "modern goings-on."[5] Is this reviewer correct? Is money a benign plaything?

A seventy-year-old man recently sought my help in understanding the rage, depression, and drug addiction of his thirty-nine-year-old son. Enormously successful in business, this man possesses the self-esteem, intelligence, and determination to have made it largely on his own. As a father, however, he was at a loss to understand why his son, who had "been given everything he ever wanted," couldn't live a healthy, productive life. This client grew up in poverty and worked fourteen- to eighteen-hour days to be acknowledged as "somebody." He candidly admits that, for him, the money quickly became secondary to his craving to be noticed and the fulfillment that this attention brought him. He was determined to leave the shame and anonymity of poverty behind. His success is chronicled in the many scrapbooks he has filled with newspaper articles extolling his rapid rise to success and power. What the articles don't mention, however, is that in his headlong rush, his children, including a mentally retarded daughter, were left to be raised by his wife and a large, transient household staff.

According to my client, his son blames him for his troubles in life. The son is understandably angry over his childhood emotional abandonment and fights constantly with his father; both father and son verbally abuse one another. A frequent client at in-patient treatment centers, the son, apparently unable to stay drug free, uses his easy access to cash to feed the addictions that began as a means to quell his fear that he couldn't accomplish anything on his own. His emotional growth suspended when he began using drugs at fourteen, he is in many ways a teenager in the body of a thirty-nine-year-old: angry, self-absorbed, irresponsible, and directionless. All along, his parents have used their money to rescue him from the consequences of outrageous, self-destructive behavior. What his parents didn't take care of, he has been able to cushion with his own income from a trust that began paying him an exorbitant sum when he turned eighteen. With so many escape routes available, he has never been forced to grow up. His overwhelming rage, turned inward over the years, has festered into a deep, addiction-driven depression, which he claims to "treat" by self-medicating. His relationship with his father is a love-hate roller coaster that fills both of them with unhappiness and despair. They have all the money in the world, but they don't have the one thing that could make them both happy—a loving, father-son relationship to nurture them both as they face their futures.

Would the effects of abject poverty—say, a father who was never home due to alcoholism, criminal justice involvement, the need to work long hours, or actual physical abandonment, and a powerless mother lost in her own misery and despair—have produced worse? Probably. Maybe the son would not even be alive today. The effects of poverty are devastating, after all, and well-documented. The negative effects of wealth, however, are not reported and need to be. In case after case, I see that the accumulation, perpetuation, and power of wealth come between the holder of that money and the life he or she might have had.

There seems to be a thin line, but one that I will try to define, between money as a gift and asset in life and money as a burden that causes unhappiness, loneliness, despair, and destruction. A recent article in *People* magazine about the life and death of Doris Duke, the "Richest Girl in the World," reveals telling evidence of the latter case. "She wanted a simple life, but 100 million dollars got in the way."[6] In future chapters, I will look at ways to recognize that "thin line" so that the abundance in your life, however it manifests itself, can be a blessing rather than a hardship.

My family was riddled by multiple divorces, affairs, alcoholism, anger, and unhappiness—not unlike many families in today's society. We have also had some wonderful success stories. The point, however, is that our money did not do what society assumes it did: it *did not* make us happier; it *did not* help us overcome our shortcomings and lead more fulfilling lives. Having money does solve the fundamental problems of survival, which, until they *are* solved, are the only problems worth consideration. The very accomplishment of surviving day to day can, for many people, bring satisfaction and fulfillment; but once a person has moved beyond mere survival, money can often take on a dangerous transformational role in people's lives. It can do great good and it can do great harm. Since most people are unaware of the inherent danger in wealth, they stumble blindly after it, incorrectly assuming that it will enhance their existence. Our culture as a whole believes that money is good and that more money is better, even as evidence to the contrary stares us in the face. Day after day, we read and hear stories in the media of addiction, despair, and death. These tales are perpetuated, exacerbated, perhaps even caused by the presence of excess wealth: O. J. and Nicole Simpson, the Menendez brothers, Pete Rose, Howard Hughes, Dennis Rodman, John Belushi. We continue to assume that money will solve *all* our problems, just as it takes care of the basic problems of survival.

Wealth, in fact, exacerbates many of our problems, making some bigger, more enduring, and much more difficult to resolve. Among the affluent, the divorces take longer and are messier—with money, once again, as the focus of the conflict. The rich who suffer from alcoholism can hide their addiction longer behind the trappings of wealth, denying their illness by invoking the power of the family name, avoiding family or professional intervention, and continuing the self-destruction that addiction promotes. Money can cushion, or entirely prevent, the descent into the life-changing, spiritual, and physical "bottoming out" that many addicts must experience in order to seek treatment. In this respect, money functions as a surrogate codependent. Ironically, it can also hasten bottoming out, as will be discussed in chapter 4.

In wealthy families, mental illnesses may be genteelly ignored. Family members who become a threat to themselves or their loved ones are quietly sent away to an expensive "resort" to "rest." Unlike the poor, should the wealthy decide to seek appropriate help, they have the ability to buy the best available. There is, however, generally great family pressure in the upper class to maintain that external appearance of perfection, never admitting that there is a problem in paradise. These strict family sanctions strengthen the individual's denial of his or her addictions or problems.

Because of my parents' flawed assumptions about the innate "goodness" of money and their subsequent lack of planning or consciousness about its use, more often than not their money became a barrier to any real happiness or intimacy in their lives. Preoccupied by and ultimately addicted to the accumulation of money and material possessions, they neglected their failing relationship. This was true as well for many of my relatives and most of the wealthy people I interviewed. The covert message we all received from our families and from society was that money was supposed to make and keep us happy. And if for some reason it didn't, then it had to be *our* fault. In addition, the money enabled us to bury the family secrets deep and well and to maintain the facade of intimacy. Misery is easily hidden behind the latched gates and the perfectly manicured gardens of the rich; all appears well. Like many wealthy families, we all blindly obeyed the powerful unspoken commandment: "Thou shalt look good, at all costs."

NOTES

1. A. Farnham, "The Children of the Rich and Famous," *Fortune,* September 1990, 112–28. Farnham deserves credit for having originated this very useful term.

2. Joyce LeBeau, "The 'Silver-Spoon Syndrome' in the Super Rich: The Pathological Linkage of Affluence and Narcissism in Family Systems," *American Journal of Psychotherapy* 42 (1988): 425.

3. Marie Kohler, "Old Money," *Milwaukee Magazine* 21 no.5 (May 1996): 59.

4. Louis Gould, "Ticket to Trouble," *New York Times Magazine,* 23 April 1995, 40.

5. Taki, "Money Does Buy Happiness," *Wall Street Journal,* Tuesday, 9 January 1996, A12.

6. Mark Goodman and Lois Armstrong, "The Burden of Riches," *People,* 15 November 1993, 69.

3

THE FAMILY FOUNDER
AND THE MYTH
OF THE AMERICAN DREAM

The enduring power of the Faust legend lies in its distillation
of the notion that all of us cut deals with our demons—the
angelic demons no less than the devilish. We steer our efforts in accordance with a given set of promises, promises
so fraught with wishing that they seem of necessity to hold
an element of magic; and whether or not we reach the fulfillment of those promises, the pursuit of them determines
our course.

LAURENCE SHAMES
The Hunger for More

While the American dream took full flight on the wings of victory following World War II, it probably began when we first became a nation. Our forefathers believed that anybody could become anything in America, and they passed that pioneer spirit on to us.

At the heart of the American dream lies the myth of equality. Anyone can become president if he works hard enough — assuming, of course, the "he" isn't a "she" and isn't nonwhite. By the mid-nineteenth century, Americans had come to believe that our country was invincible. Firm in the conviction that democratic capitalism was the only viable form of government and commerce, we worked to establish our new and, we believed, better path in the world.

Following World War II, our self-confidence and optimism were unsurpassed. America had never lost a war. Wealth came easily — and, it seemed, rightfully — to a young nation full of pride. The national pain and malaise created by the Great Depression seemed firmly behind us. There appeared to be more than enough prosperity for everyone. The poor were ignored or forgotten; the United States was seen as a rich country, and the dream of affluence pervaded it in a manner that was historically unmatched by any nation in the world. Americans quickly adapted to the idea that a socially correct image meant having two cars in every garage, a chicken in every pot, and women whose only roles in life were those of wife and mother. Not only could we do and be anything we set our minds to, but getting rich doing it became part of the goal and, finally, the goal itself.

In this context, the ideological linkage between profits and human purpose solidified and became an increasingly and unapologetically conscious belief system. Business, and the burgeoning new technologies and foreign markets that drove business, became the ascendant cultural idol. Making money became an act of patriotism. It was during this period, in 1953, that my grand-father C. E. Wilson, then nominee for secretary of defense, uttered his famous (or infamous, depending on your point of view) decla-ration that, "What's good for the country is good for General Motors and vice versa." Elsewhere, a large insurance company president solemnly proclaimed to his employees, "All that we de-sire can come only from profits." The quote was printed on the company's coffee mugs.

In the wake of this unparalleled prosperity, we became arro-gant, taking our successes and our material comforts for granted. As a nation, we quickly developed the false sense of entitlement that is characteristic of affluenza. On the world stage, we began to believe that our country *deserved* to be treated differently, better than others. We felt entitled to live in great material luxury, not necessarily because we had worked hard to earn it, but simply because of who we were. Money came easily and quickly; we ex-pected our incomes and standards of living to continue to soar.

This false optimism and sense of entitlement can currently be seen in the attitude of the baby boomers, who, as a group, have made few financial plans for retirement. A recent article in a Mid-western newspaper stated that baby boomers are saving only one-third of what they will need to maintain their current lifestyle in retirement.

Most of us have an idea of how much it will cost to ensure a comfortable old age in a changing economy, and yet we do little about it, as though our needs will magically be met. We watch as the Social Security system begins to weaken and collapse; yet like teenagers, we believe that we are invincible and that losing this tra-ditional bulwark is something that could never happen to us.

Economic projections and the falling post–baby boomer birth-rate tell a different story, however. In a few decades, workers will need to contribute about half of their paychecks to support the Social Security system, given the number of elderly people who will be relying on it by then. In spite of such facts, we live in a state of perennial financial denial, continuing to believe that somehow, without effort or sacrifice, our country will self-correct and return to its rightful state of affluence.

The view many Americans hold that they are unique and special is only a larger manifestation of the belief system at work in adult children of dysfunctional families (ACDFs). This self-defeating condition is widely known as "terminal uniqueness." Terminal uniqueness is a characteristic of addicts, adult children of addicts, and affluenza sufferers that makes people feel as if they are set apart from the rest of humankind, that they are special. It distances them, encourages them to believe they are different from everyone else, and therefore severely impedes emotional development, particularly the creation of intimacy. In essence, this attitude freezes people in isolation and keeps them from growing. For example, seeing oneself as essentially the same as other people would, for the wealthy individual, create a connection to the rest of humanity, making them equals and creating the possibility of community or even intimacy—a thought unconsciously too terrifying for many ACDFs to handle. Rather than deal with reality, Americans have continued to turn to the allure of the American dream fantasy.

During the eighties, the Reagan years, the American people reached an all-time frenzied high in their determination to accumulate wealth and possessions. A popular T-shirt read, "Whoever dies with the most toys, wins." The quiet, subtle handling of inherited wealth was replaced by proud, outspoken displays of newly acquired money. In the world of fashion, the conservative, tailored styles favored for so long by the well-heeled rich were brashly replaced with sparkling, brightly colored sequins, and a booming market developed for "faux" jewels. Many of the old guard found this new attitude vulgar, but before the end of the decade, both the old money and the nouveau riche swirled together in ballrooms across the country. Now, as the middle class becomes smaller, the poor poorer, and the very rich very much richer, people continue to cling desperately to the fading American dream.

The Myth

"People tend to get either neurotic or crazy or obsessive in the way that the culture allows it. The people who have the greatest success in our society are the people who can get the most in each generation, in each culture period," according to New York psychotherapist Leonora Tint.[1] Everywhere you look—on magazine covers, on billboards, and in soap opera story lines—you see images reinforcing the belief that money can and does buy happiness. Most of us, if confronted with this proposition, would deny that we believe anything so naive and simplistic; yet many still secretly hope the formula is true and daydream about achieving total fulfillment when "our ship comes in" or upon winning the lottery. Those like myself who have experienced much sorrow because of wealth, however, unequivocally know that the myth which equates money with happiness and fulfillment is an outright lie. Unfortunately, this is a lesson long in the learning. For the majority of the newly affluent, the road still looks smooth, and they still believe money will guarantee their safe passage.

Only pain and disillusionment lie at the end of a life in which the sole measure of success is how much money is left in the bank. Mature and emotionally healthy older people, as they near their transition to death, speak much less of the material things in their lives and more of their relationships and what they have learned in the process of living; they strive for an understanding and a spiritual peace with their god, however they might define that term.

It's the old rhetorical question: "How many people, lying on their death beds, express the regret that they should have spent more time at the office?" In the past several years, as I watched my father slowly choose death over life, I was struck by his growing detachment from the material world. Although concerned that his financial affairs be in order, he turned less and less to the daily reports of the stock market, and more to reminiscence of his significant relationships.

But the realization of what is important in life comes not only to the very old; it also pushes persistently beneath the surface of our culture. The malaise that currently grips our country comes not from the fact that we don't have enough wealth, but from a terrifying knowledge that has begun to enter our consciousness that we have based our entire lives, our entire culture and way of being, on the wrong premise. In our naiveté, our addictive greed, and our separation from our spiritual source, we have wandered farther and farther down the wrong road. When we awaken long enough to glimpse this frightening truth, it is all too easy to frantically reach for another "fix" to numb the pain: another house, another spouse, another child, another car, another dress, another ring, another lie.

We try to tell ourselves that when we have enough we'll be fulfilled and happy—but how much, exactly, is *enough?* The definition of this word is relative, and every person has a different answer. Really having enough is a sacred state of mind that has nothing to do with money. Many contemporary spiritual leaders—Marianne Williamson, Deepak Chopra, Marsha Sinetar, and others—will tell you that when you believe deep in your heart that *you* are enough, then you will have all that you need.

Most people in our culture never reach this place of inner peace. Many who have either inherited or accumulated what they hoped would be enough money and material possessions must either face the horrible truth that that is not what life is about after all, or increase their level of denial to obliterate the truth. It takes incredible amounts of energy and time to maintain that level of denial. As those who have spent their lives as workaholics bent on achieving success at any cost, often at the sacrifice of family and other relationships, reach midlife and beyond, the horror of what they've done often becomes more difficult to ignore. Numbing that pain takes more and more money, more material possessions, and more drugs and alcohol. In light of this, it is no surprise that we are a society of addicts. Money, with its indiscriminate transformational power for good or for evil, is often used to supply the latest and strongest aids to denial.

From every addiction—be it drugs, alcohol, work, or the worship of materialism—there is recovery. Across the country, Twelve Step programs continue to grow to meet the needs of those individuals who are willing to face the darkness within themselves. For those who are disillusioned with the Twelve Step process, a wide variety of other spiritual and emotional support systems are available.

Religion has pruned itself, growing and blossoming, creating a myriad of new and fascinating combinations of the old standbys. One can now choose among a variety of New Age spiritual paths, as well as from the many manifestations of the old-time religions—Eastern, Western, Northern and Southern! There are motivational seminars, conferences, and lectures that are spiritually based, business based, or both. More and more people are becoming aware of a number of practices, such as Yoga, that nurture and discipline the body, mind, and spirit. There is, I assure you, something for you if you are willing to take the time to look for it.

The Family Founder

Unfortunately, the cure is out of sight and out of mind during the initial headlong rush to accumulate wealth. The addictive, medicating quality of money is particularly visible in, and strengthened by, the hectic lifestyle of the Family Founder, the person who makes the original fortune. (I use the pronoun *he* here because all of the founders I have encountered — personally, in my research, and in my practice — have been male. This is by no means any indication that there have not been, or could not be, female Family Founders.) The Family Founder lives for the newness and excitement of the pursuit of the American dream, believing that catching the brass ring will make him happy. Since he is the first member of the family to "make it" to this stratospheric plane, it does not matter if he is vaguely aware that others have failed to find fulfillment in wealth. After a while, it no longer matters that filling in that big financial scorecard with victory after victory means neglecting or altering other parts of his life, sometimes irreparably.

For Family Founders, the process of earning the fortune brings tremendous ego and self-esteem-building implications that will always be absent from the lives of those who merely inherit their wealth. Founders are secure in the knowledge that they have earned their money and therefore amply deserve it. They invariably believe they have the right to display it, spend it, save it, sprinkle it from the window of a skyscraper if they want to. The money is undeniably theirs, to do with as they please. Founders experience a tremendous sense of pride and accomplishment in the knowledge that they have made it on their own.

On the other hand, families such as the Kennedys, the Astors, and the Rockefellers, long familiar with the pitfalls of immense wealth, look at their largess as an immense responsibility, a burden to be borne dutifully rather than a source of pleasure or fun. In *The Rockefellers: An American Dynasty*, Peter Collier and David Horowitz wrote, "Instead of wealth coming, however obliquely, as a reward for individual effort, the individual would pay a life-time debt of service to the wealth itself and thus earn it after the fact."[2]

Personality Traits of the Family Founder

Family Founders often share several personality traits. These traits both contribute to their high level of success and cause the many personal and relational problems they experience with friends, family, and associates.

THE "NEVER-ENOUGH" MENTALITY: ADDICTIVE / COMPULSIVE BEHAVIOR

As we have seen, part of the American dream is the belief that anyone who works hard enough can strike it rich. Rich is "good," something to dedicate your life to, something to strive for with your heart and soul, something that many Americans spend their entire lives trying to achieve. Although many hold the American dream to be valid, the majority fall far short of attaining it.

What characteristics make one person reach for the brass ring and the next person content to simply ride the merry-go-round? A close look at the giant moneymakers reveals that almost all of them have addictive/compulsive personalities. Landi writes, "The real compulsion behind the never-enough mentality—and the danger isn't limited to the loaded—isn't having money, it's making it."[3] When J. D. Rockefeller was once asked how much would be enough, he replied, "Just a little bit more." The addiction is to the "game" itself, to the internal chemistry of arousal and the psychological rewards that winning the game provides.

The very ambitious are driven by an internal measure of success, an uncompromising set of standards, the need to be perfect. Money is simply the scorecard with which to measure their success. During my interview with Peter Buffet, son of financier Warren Buffet, I was dumbfounded to learn that Peter was not aware of his family's immense wealth until after he got out of college. He pointed out that his father was not interested in spending the money, only in making it. Thus, they lived a relatively "normal" upper-middle-class life.

The acquisition of possessions and money is, at the very least, a way to distract us from the things that aren't working in our lives: unhealed relationships with parents, failing relationships with spouses or children, or extreme loneliness and isolation. At worst, it becomes a driving, all-consuming addiction requiring extensive intervention and treatment to change. Either way wealth and ambition are distancing tools, and keep us successfully at arm's length from potentially intimate relationships. This is where the "sins" of the father — the Family Founder — can become the "sins" of the son. If our parents are emotionally detached from us, then we are likely to unconsciously choose that distancing method also. Those who have been abandoned, emotionally or physically, in that most intimate of relationships with their parents often make an unconscious decision at a deep gut level to never let themselves be hurt again. When people begin to experience feelings that remind them, consciously or unconsciously, of that long-ago love and rejection, fear takes over, making them unable to continue to develop what might be a truly intimate, loving relationship.

Many Family Founders develop their wealth obsessions out of a sincere desire to take care of those they love. This is not just true of the very wealthy, but for a whole generation of men and women who were absent from their homes in order to provide for their families. One woman told me how her father, who came from a background of emotional and financial poverty, worked day and night for decades to establish his own business and make it grow. He may only have achieved the status of the upper-middle class, but his family still saw very little of him; yet all of this work was done because he loved them and wanted them to have everything he never had. This leads to a tragic inversion of values that can create multiple generations of emotionally (and physically) absent parents. In trying to provide their children with the material things they never received, they neglected to give them the things they *had* received: their parents' time and attention. Those who grow up in emotional and financial poverty may find it difficult as adults to realize there are ways of loving one's family that go far beyond the bestowal of wealth.

"TYPE T" PERSONALITIES: THRILL SEEKERS

University of Wisconsin at Madison psychologist Frank Farley calls compulsive moneymakers "Type T" personalities, thrill seekers who get high on risk-taking. Type Ts get their kicks from any kind of risky exploit, positive or negative, from the big deal at the board table to the big deal in the drug world. Type Ts are constantly pushing the limits; they are rule breakers by nature. Many of the people who attained prominence throughout history were Type Ts.

This drive to walk on the edge, seemingly inborn in some people, also produces an adrenaline/endorphin-altered state similar to a "runner's high." The chemical rush and energy experienced during an actual business deal can be powerful. Endorsed by society and rewarded by financial gain, is it any wonder that these types return again and again to the boardrooms where they got their first "fix"? We are talking about men and women who are trying to fill an inner void with outer resources, a losing and frustrating battle. I remember clearly the feeling of exhilaration following one particularly confrontational real estate negotiation with which I was involved. I "won" and my opponent lost, and for several days the false sense of superiority generated from this experience fed my faltering ego.

The game of one-upmanship, however, is a dangerous and alienating one. When Family Founders express their true feelings, they often admit it is pretty lonely at the top. In an interview, Barbara Walters once asked Ted Turner, "What do you mean by success? What, to you, is being successful?" His response: "Well, I think it's kind of an empty bag, to tell the truth. To a large degree it is. But you have to get there to really know that. I mean, money doesn't buy happiness and neither does honors or position and awards or trophies."[4]

NARCISSISM AND DIFFERENTIATION:
THE NEED TO BE SPECIAL

Many of the very rich, particularly the Family Founders, suffer from extreme narcissism, an acute, almost pathological need to be special.[5] Wealthy men quite often attract women of great beauty who are accustomed to adulation and tend to be aloof and self-absorbed—women, in short, who themselves suffer from narcissism.[6] These people have developed neither a strong ego nor a healthy sense of self-esteem, so they act out, attempting to gain attention through extreme financial success or outrageous positive or negative behavior. It is this need that drove the philanthropy of Andrew Carnegie, the Kennedys, Andrew Mellon, and the Vanderbilts as well as the ostentatious display of Donald Trump and Leona Helmsley. The whole point of such behavior, however, is not altruism or trouble making, but the need to appear different from others.[7] The Hunts and Ross Perot of Texas, and the Huffingtons of California are prime examples of how people get hooked on money, in part, for the notoriety it provides them. "Money came ahead of sleeping and eating," *Fortune* magazine reported of Ivan Boesky. "He seemed to have few interests outside of making money," *New York* magazine claimed, referring to Harry Helmsley. "There is something about being a Hunt—you're never rich enough," writes Dallas journalist A. C. Green in the *New York Times Magazine.*[8]

WORKAHOLISM

Looking at greed, the need to always make more, as an addiction puts the problem into a clinical rather than a moral framework. In a *New York Times* editorial, Jay Rohrlich, a Wall Street psychiatrist, described greed as one of the key characteristics that was ruining the lives of his patients.[9] As Twelve Step programs and other programs of healing became more and more popular during the eighties, this compulsive behavior or never-enough mentality became labeled "workaholism": an addiction to activity and an addiction to money. Clinical treatment facilities all over the world now offer in-patient and out-patient services for workaholism, among other addictions.

Popular theory claims that a financially impoverished childhood lies behind the self-made person's pathological fear of never having enough. Yet it seems far more likely that emotional impoverishment is the fuel that stokes the fires of ambition. Beyond the necessities of survival, I have not had a client nor heard of anyone whose emotional problems stemmed from the deprivation of material possessions as a child. By the time a Family Founder with a Type T personality comes to me for therapy, his level of misery and discomfort is so high that it is not hard to discern the underlying causes. In my experience, the need to succeed at all costs always stems from feelings of inadequacy coupled with low self-esteem and lack of self-confidence.

Albert Einstein and Winston Churchill are two examples of Type Ts whose need to expand the parameters of their existence resulted in positive change for the world at large. Others, such as Ivan Boesky and his partner in crime Martin Siegel, succumbing to the dangerous and addictive allure of money, are Type Ts whose effect on our money-consciousness has been both eye-opening and decidedly negative. (Ivan Boesky was a Wall Street arbitrageur worth an estimated $200 million, who went to jail convicted of insider trading. Martin Siegel was a young millionaire take-over specialist who received large sums of cash from Boesky in exchange for confidential information on Siegel's clients.)

I have one client, George, who is in his mid-sixties, divorced, a practicing alcoholic and "successful" workaholic. He was the oldest son of a poor, depression-era family. He recently told me that he was the only one of the four children in his family who was whipped with a belt. His two sisters were spared because of their gender, and his younger brother escaped the abuse due to chronic asthma and the protection of his mother. George said he sometimes wondered if his father whipped only him because he was worse than the others and maybe he didn't like him as much. Then he shook his head, as though to discard such a thought, and said, "Oh, but I know that wasn't really true." Such rationalization and denial comes easily to an adult, but to a child being beaten, there is only the reality of the pain.

Following his traumatic childhood, George went on to marry a wealthy woman who helped him start an extremely successful chain of hardware stores. However, he is convinced that he would have never made it without her money, in spite of evidence to the contrary. Undermined, beaten, and abused by his father and further emasculated by his wife's money, George continues to work and drink in a futile attempt to quell his never-enough mentality and his feelings of inadequacy and inferiority. In his case, and many others, it is not only never-enough money, it is a pervasive belief that they themselves are never enough—good enough, smart enough, handsome or pretty enough, thin enough, successful enough, and so on.

Emotionally deprived, compulsive moneymakers are driven by workaholism and the need for differentiation to work long exhausting hours away from home. As their intimate relationships deteriorate, it becomes easier and finally preferable to stay at work rather than face the disappointment and anger at home. As they become more proficient at their jobs, and less proficient at cultivating and maintaining intimate relationships, they begin to choose work over nearly everything else.

When these men have children, they leave them in the care of their wives or servants. When the wives are also narcissistic, themselves the product of emotional deprivation, they are obviously poorly equipped to be competent, loving mothers. These women often require constant positive mirroring for themselves and are frequently in competition with their own daughters.[10] As these men and women become accustomed to the immediate gratification that their increasing wealth provides, they begin to find the often delayed satisfaction of parenting unacceptable and impossible to imagine. Unlike their less-affluent counterparts, they can afford to "buy out" of parenting.

Seeking to climb the social ladder as they climb the corporate ladder, they search the world of "old money" for role models to shape their behavior. Since it is not only acceptable but also a sign of affluence to afford surrogate care for one's children, they are quick to join the world of nannies, au pairs, and boarding schools.

THE "BUY OUT" PRINCIPLE:
AN INABILITY TO DELAY GRATIFICATION
AND TOLERATE FRUSTRATION

The characteristics that most hinder and interfere with recovery from affluenza are the inability to delay gratification and tolerate frustration. The destructiveness of these two traits cannot be overemphasized. Although these characteristics may not necessarily be present during the early years of financial accumulation, they seem to grow in direct proportion to the balance in the bank account of the Family Founder. Seduced by the power of money to make things happen immediately and at will, the Founder and his family begin to develop a destructive false sense of entitlement. This unattractive trait is thus created during the Family Founder's lifetime and passed down to subsequent generations. When someone uses the word *spoiled* in reference to a wealthy person, I believe they are most often unconsciously referring to this characteristic.

In a deeper sense, the inability to delay gratification or deal with frustration is a form of black-and-white thinking. Individuals with such a characteristic see relationships, jobs, challenges, and problems to be solved as "all or nothing." This perfectionism drives them to believe that if they can't do these things perfectly, they can't attempt them at all. The affluenza/dysfunctional trait of grandiosity slips neatly into the equation to further distance an individual from the reality of the situation. What becomes less apparent to the Family Founder as success alters his perspective, and equally lost to his descendants, is the knowledge of how to take the little everyday steps of living. It is this patience and persistence that leads to a productive, truly successful, fulfilling life. How the loss of this skill affects the subsequent generations will be discussed in detail in chapter 4.

THE NEED TO CONTROL: FEAR

Many Family Founders and their heirs have an intense need to control the people and situations around them. Although it would appear at first glance that this need is an extension of the above-mentioned inability to delay gratification and tolerate frustration, it is frequently a function of fear. If the individuals are of the never-enough mentality, it is quite possible that they are actually struggling with feelings of inferiority rather than superiority. This being the case, their desire and attempts to control situations and people around them are driven by fear. They have no faith that without their manipulation, the situation might resolve in their favor or that it might be done with their best interest in mind. They don't believe that anyone could like them, respect them, or care enough about a relationship with them to seek their advice or listen to them. As children who had little or no control over their fate, they now believe that the only way the outcome could possibly be good is if they control it. Because most of their emotional needs went unmet during their childhoods, they believe that they must grab what they want or need in no uncertain terms.

One of the most vivid examples of this need to control is the Family Founder's way of handling his death and the dispensation of his fortune. Preoccupied with the accumulation and maintenance of money for much of their lives, Family Founders are forced to concentrate even harder on control or how to let go of it and the organization of their estates with the encroachment of old age and impending death. By controlling their estates, wealthy people can sometimes convince themselves that they have some control over death. Their fear of dying can be ignored or delayed, for at least a short time, by the illusion of control. At a time when one would hope that relationships and feelings might begin to take on more importance, Family Founders are called upon to make final and extensive financial decisions that will greatly affect their loved ones whom they choose to leave their money to. Because they have spent most of their lives more comfortable in relationships with their money than with their families, it is no surprise that they frequently continue this lonely existence until death.

The death of a parent or close relative is heartbreaking and difficult, but wealth can make it worse—or at least more complex. If the amount of money involved has been kept a secret, as is frequently the case in dysfunctional affluent homes, then the inheritor may be surprised and thrown into further confusion. Healthy grieving may be postponed or repressed in favor of focusing on the powerful charisma and pleasant thoughts of riches to come. Fantasies of luxurious vacations and fabulous shopping sprees are obviously alluring and seductive and become strong competition for the feelings of sadness and loss that are a healthy and appropriate response to the death of a loved one.

Not surprisingly, along with the confusion and allure of the impending wealth come feelings of guilt. This guilt is perpetuated and intensified by any unresolved emotions that the inheritor might have toward his or her benefactor. Accustomed to controlling and manipulating the lives of family members before his death, the Family Founder often attempts to do so even from the grave. If the stipulations and conditions of the will and trusts have not been discussed previously, the inheritors are left with the difficult task of interpreting these meanings on their own, adding anger at the ongoing manipulation to the already present guilt and confusion. Over time, this ambivalence may become shame as the memories of the Founder's control habits begin to blur and fade. Survivors begin to ask themselves over and over again, "How could I have felt so angry toward him, been so mean to him," and so on. The interplay of unresolved feelings and the creation of shame will be examined and discussed in chapter 6. The obvious and difficult answer to this legacy of confusion and pain is for the Family Founder and any potential heirs to discuss the estate planning, resolve their differences, and make peace before it is too late.

How the Myth of the American Dream
Hurts All of Us, Rich or Poor

An individual does not have to be a Family Founder, the creator of a vast fortune, to suffer from the traits described above. The overly ambitious—in fact, anyone who worships the almighty dollar—is prone to addictive/compulsive behaviors, physical and emotional unavailability, never-enough mentality, narcissism, and the illusion that money buys freedom from pain. The children of anyone of such beliefs will suffer many of the same consequences as the children of affluence.

Think carefully about how you spend your time. Do you work late every night to achieve a standard of living that someone else set for you? Is this level of material success really what you want and need? Have you lost your family and friends in the process of getting ahead? More important, have you lost yourself? Everyone must strive for balance in his or her life. To stay healthy, we need to take as much care with our souls and spirits as we do with balancing our checkbooks.

The perpetuation of the American dream hurts all of us, regardless of our socioeconomic level. Of course having a certain amount of money frees one from a level of poverty and hunger that no one should ever have to experience. The never-enough mentality of the Family Founder, however, feeds a culture-wide gestalt of scarcity and fear. As individuals, we respond to this by hoarding what we *do* have, instead of sharing our abundance. As fear and violence in our country increase, we hold on even tighter. This bunker mentality manifests not only in the walled communities of the very rich, but also in the rise of civilian militias and other hate groups. We have become our own worst enemy. Even though the U.S. is the richest country in the world in terms of per-capita purchasing power, it is nineteenth to last on a scale that measures a country's social and economic well-being. In these important respects, we are last among the developed nations, with a poverty rate double that of every industrialized European nation except the U.K.[11]

What begins as a dream often becomes, within one short generation, a nightmare, one that subsequent generations seem destined to be tormented by again and again. It is my most fervent prayer and deepest hope that we as a nation can create a new dream, one based on the knowledge that there *is* enough of everything: enough money, enough housing, enough food. This realization will only come to us when we can begin to break this cycle of affluenza that threatens to destroy us, our children, and our communities.

Our first step is to look inside ourselves for affirmation, to value the internal reward of rising self-esteem based on qualities such as generosity of spirit, emotional maturity, and the ability to experience joy, inner peace, and contentment. The best things in life are not things. When we learn to value ourselves simply for who we are, when we learn to love our children simply because they are our children, when we learn to radically shift our priorities and focus our energies and resources on helping those less fortunate than we are, we will be on our way to creating a new American dream.

NOTES

1. Ann Landi, "When Having Everything Isn't Enough," *Psychology Today* (April 1989): 27–30.

2. John Taylor, *Circus of Ambition* (New York: Warner Books, 1989), 4.

3. Landi, "When Having Everything Isn't Enough," 27–30.

4. Ted Turner, interview by Barbara Walters, *20/20*, ABC News, 23 February 1990.

5. Steven Berglas, *The Success Syndrome: Hitting Bottom When You Reach the Top* (New York: Plenum Press, 1986), 33.

6. Joyce LeBeau, "The 'Silver-Spoon' Syndrome' in the Super Rich: The Pathological Linkage of Affluence and Narcissism in Family Systems," *American Journal of Psychotherapy* 42 (1988): 426–36.

7. Berglas, *The Success Syndrome,* 48–49.

8. Landi, "When Having Everything Isn't Enough," 28–29.

9. Ibid., 29

10. LeBeau, "The 'Silver-Spoon Syndrome' in the Super Rich," 426.

11. "Can You Ever Have Enough?" *More Than Money* no. 4 (1994): 15.

4

POOR LITTLE RICH KIDS: THE HIDDEN LEGACY OF WEALTH

For all its undeniable glory, the money involves hazards that all rich kids have to face. It is like some magic sword: it gives the holder rare powers, but only the mightiest warriors can keep from being nicked themselves by the blade.

JOHN SEDGWICK
Rich Kids

THE LAST CHAPTER DESCRIBED SOME OF THE characteristics of the Family Founder: ambition, a need to be perfect, an uncompromising set of standards, a never-enough mentality, and an addictive/compulsive personality. During my interviews with the heirs of the founders, I was struck by the similar descriptions they gave of their fathers—and mothers. While driving themselves mercilessly, Family Founders and their spouses also expect their children to excel in everything they do: sports, music, art, academics, and strict adherence to social customs and mores. This can create a crippling pressure for young people, pressure to look good, behave with intelligence and self-confidence, and achieve—at any cost. One must attend the "right" schools, get excellent grades, marry the "right" person from a socially acceptable family, have a powerful and distinguished career if one is male, and be thin, beautiful, ever-smiling, and entertaining if one is female.

Concerned primarily with how their children appear to others, the Family Founders are preoccupied with their own unrelenting schedules and are seldom present to witness their children's attempts to please them. By imposing a rigid, unrealistic, and highly structured lifestyle upon their children, they rob them of their childhoods.

As family conflict and stress build, fathers, mothers, and children alike frequently turn to alcohol, drugs, sex, gambling, and other potentially addictive, harmful behaviors in a futile effort to escape or ameliorate the strain. As already mentioned, a major factor in this family tension is the disillusioning failure of the American dream which promises that money will deliver happiness. When it doesn't, what were once occasional pleasures can be transformed into addictions or other forms of destructive behavior.

Families, friends, acquaintances, and fans politely look the other way as other crimes, illnesses, and tragedies are allowed to occur inside the homes of the very rich. Rampant addictions, spousal abuse, physical and psychological abuse, and untreated mental illness are but a few examples. In homes where wealth excuses any type of outrageous or destructive behavior in the parents, and where love, self-control, and self-esteem are not modeled for the children, dysfunctional characteristics and personality traits are passed from generation to generation.

The lonely child of chronically absent parents will most likely become an adult who struggles to find enough love to fill the emotional void created in childhood. In unhealthy rich families, however, children usually realize that their parents are absent not because of economic necessity, but because they choose not to be there. Furthermore, these children almost always internalize the implications of these absences.

These implications are several and harmful. If you believe that your parents cared so little for you that they didn't bother to spend time with you, despite potentially infinite opportunity, how as an adult could you ever believe that *anyone* could ever really love you? Furthermore, showered with toys, lessons, and the trappings of social status rather than with time and love; raised by servants who never said "no," given no guidelines for appropriate behavior—how does one become an adult who can create realistic, healthy emotional and physical boundaries in one's relationships with others *or* with oneself? It is little wonder that the children of financial giants often grow up with severe emotional and psychological problems. They were raised in an environment that placed a higher value on material satisfaction than on emotional sustenance. Love, after all, is not about money; it is about nurturance: time spent talking, playing, touching, laughing, and crying together. Being given everything that money can buy is no substitute for being treasured for being yourself. Affluence and the single-minded pursuit of wealth not only accentuate problems that already exist in any dysfunctional family, they also create many additional ones.

Empty Childhoods:
Lack of Love, Missing Parents, and Low Self-Esteem

What is the root cause of these problems? And how does money contribute to the severity of how they manifest in adulthood? I have many clients who suffer not only from affluenza but also from a variety of obsessive-compulsive tendencies, disorders, and/ or addictions. What many of these patients have in common is parents who were emotionally unavailable, unable to nurture their children in a consistent, healthy manner. The degree of dysfunctional behavior or symptoms these individuals display is often directly proportional to the severity of their emotional deprivation in childhood. The emotional and/or physical abandonment of a child, for whatever reason, can be devastating.

Some affluent families, although materially satiated, suffer a pattern of emotional deprivation strikingly similar to that of underprivileged families. Both rich and poor children suffer from the emotional effects of parents who are frequently absent. Father-child contact among the wealthy is often almost nonexistent due to professional and recreational preoccupations. When Dad is at work or "networking," and Mother is consumed with social activities, there is no time remaining for parenting. Raised by servants, these children have little knowledge of family or cultural values except what can be inferred. Like their poverty-stricken peers, they frequently develop a distorted sense of right and wrong, learning to grab what they want, when they want it, in whatever manner is available to them. Because no one is there to teach them healthy coping strategies, they reach for "quick fixes" to compensate for the emotional instability in their lives.

What sorts of behaviors and deficiencies are common among children who grow up with absent fathers? In his book *What Happened to Their Kids?*, Malcolm Forbes tells the story of the oil

tycoon Jean Paul Getty who had five sons from five different marriages and rarely saw any of them. By the time Getty died in 1976,
two of his sons were already dead, one from a drug overdose. His
other three sons had long since been pushed out of his cherished
oil empire. As is often the case, his sons mirrored the dysfunctional behavior of their father, each succeeding father-son relationship as distant and strained as the last. In 1981, after a night
of swallowing alcohol, methadone, and Valium, J. Paul Getty III
suffered a stroke and fell into a coma. He regained consciousness
six weeks later but was blind, paralyzed, and could not speak.
Martine, Paul's girlfriend since he was sixteen, says that now
Paul's son and his stepdaughter "cuddle up with him in bed and
talk to him all the time and tell him what they have been doing.
Now they have him all the time and they are happy about that."[1]
It took a terrible tragedy to make this Getty father "available" to
his children.

Julilly Kohler, of the Kohler Co. fortune (located in Kohler,
Wisconsin—named after the family), is very aware of the effect
that absent parents have had on her own ability to parent. Because
of this awareness, she is making a valiant attempt to break the dysfunctional generational cycle.

> My children are probably the hardest issue in my life. That's
> where I'm spending my time and energy right now; to under-
> stand myself well enough to learn how to break the cycle, to not
> do it again. I realized that I was doing with my professional life
> what my mother had done with her social life. I didn't have time
> for them. My kids were always secondary to a client or a court
> case or a convention I had to go to. [I had] fifty million excuses
> why I wasn't there for them.[2]

Rich or poor, children who do not receive the love and attention
they need in their formative years often become adults who dis-

play a high degree of neediness in their relationships, an inability to sustain intimacy, low self-esteem, low self-worth, lack of self-confidence, an inability to delay gratification and tolerate frustration, and depression leading to high rates of suicide. (In 1994, 5,350 Americans between the ages of fifteen and twenty-four committed suicide—the third leading cause of death for that age group.)[3]

As discussed earlier, a major factor in the abandonment issues for adults raised in wealthy families is the ongoing succession of paid in-house childcare. Joyce LeBeau brings up an interesting possible reason for this rapid turnover of caretakers. Affluent parents, although themselves often uninterested in the tasks of parenting, are likely to become jealous and feel threatened if their children become attached to the nurse or nanny.[4] To appease their fear of being replaced, even in a role they are unable or unwilling to fulfill, they fire the hired caretakers, thus depriving the children of a stable parent figure and ensuring the perpetuation of the effects of emotional abandonment on yet another generation. With each successive loss of a loving and attentive caretaker, the child becomes less willing and less able to attach and commit to a lasting relationship for fear that it will also be taken away. The trauma is heightened by the fact that one person the child loves (the nanny) is being sent away by an even more important love object (the parent). The children learn to believe it is not safe to love: "Whomever I love leaves or is sent away. I must be unlovable or they would stay. I will not love or be loved."

LeBeau concludes that people who have such empty childhoods are likely to develop a narcissistic character pathology. These children, in turn, become ineffectual or absent parents, perpetuating an affluent type of narcissism LeBeau calls "the silver-spoon" syndrome. This syndrome will be discussed in greater detail later in this chapter.

Social and Emotional Isolation

Children of affluence are set apart from their less-affluent peers by geographical and social differences. They often attend private schools and boarding schools during the school year, and are sent to special recreational camps in the summer. The way they dress, the language they use, the cars they drive (and the fact that they *have* cars to drive) — essentially everything about their exterior appearance and behavior serves to isolate them within their own subculture. Although a sense of isolation is not abnormal for children of any socioeconomic group, especially adolescents, these distancing factors may begin sooner in the lives of wealthy children due to the early regimentation of their days.

In addition, the earliest socialization experiences of children of affluence are often limited to paid adults who frequently have little vested interest in their actual character development. As a result, interpersonal relationships may take on a removed, slightly surreal quality. Having never experienced an emotionally intimate relationship, wealthy children stumble into adulthood with no knowledge of how to love or be loved, yearning for an experience they can't even identify. P. Edidin describes an affluent young woman named Sybil who clearly grasped this dilemma:

> Eventually she could accept in a limited way that her own feelings of isolation and unimportance . . . were more properly to be understood as symptoms of her early deprivation, and not as eternal verities. "But what," she then poignantly inquired, "am I to substitute for all that I didn't get? If I didn't have a mother to whom I could feel like I counted, who will I have then?"[5]

Lack of Personal Identity

Being raised by surrogate caretakers rather than parents causes another problem: because family roles, values, concerns, and expectations often fail to be transmitted, or are transmitted incorrectly, these children frequently fail to develop a strong, healthy sense of personal identity. Growing up separated from other children, sheltered to the point of boredom, they become unable to form interests or to identify those activities in life that might give them some healthy personal satisfaction. Where emotionally healthy parents would guide and support their children in choosing activities based on their natural talents and inclinations, this is not always the case with hired help. During their developmental years, these children also fail to receive the parental mirroring of their behavior. Mirroring is the psychological process in which one person (the parent) reflects back to another (the child) what they hear or see them feeling. It is crucial for healthy psychological growth and identification of feelings.

Given the narcissistic personality traits that are common among the parents of wealthy children, however, hired caretakers may actually be better role models and purveyors of mental health than the parents. In her best-selling book *The Drama of the Gifted Child,* psychologist Alice Miller says these children are "usually freer to develop in their own way" because they are less often forced to become a reflection of their parents' narcissism.[6]

All of the adults I interviewed remember at least some of their nurses and nannies with great joy and affection. Peter Buffet, son of the multibillionaire financier Warren Buffet, still sends his childhood nanny money each month. Julilly Kohler says, "The butler and the maid were probably much closer to me than my own friends. They were surrogate parents. . . . There was some real affection there. In many ways they were the emotional anchors of my childhood and I don't know what I would have done without them."

Emotional Abandonment Combined with
Emotional or Physical Incest

Sometimes children of affluence experience emotional abandonment and emotional or physical incest. The latter occurs when the parent is gratifying his or her own unmet needs for intimacy, physical or emotional, at the expense of the child's needs and emotional security.

A client of mine provides a prime example of emotional incest. This young man, Dan, has lost both of his parents, emotionally and as role models—his father through death and his mother due to her inability to deal with her husband's death in a healthy way. The mother, unable to face her grief alone or find sufficient support among friends or through therapy, began to keep Dan home from high school for a variety of reasons that made it impossible for the school to intervene. This action has caused Dan to visibly regress emotionally and scholastically. Not only is his own grief going unaddressed, but he is also being exploited emotionally to take care of his mother's loss. Dan has been doubly abandoned, physically by his father and emotionally by his mother.

Discussed in greater detail in chapter 5, Gloria Steinem presents a compelling argument to suggest that there is a higher rate of incest in affluent, powerful households. When one takes into consideration the false sense of entitlement and narcissistic, "I want what I want when I want it" attitude frequently found in the wealthy, it is not hard to believe that she might be right.

"We have read about rich girls who were victims of incestuous relationships, from fictional Nicole Diver in Fitzgerald's *Tender Is the Night* to the real Edie Sedgwick of the 1960s," writes Steinem. She goes on to point out that pre-feminism, Freudian bias held incest to be a fantasy of the victim and the fate of only the poor. "We now have reason to believe that Freud falsified evidence of the prevalence of incest precisely because society would not accept the degree to which its practitioners were solid patriarchs of the middle and upper class."[7]

One-Dimensional Memories

The survival need to repress painful memories from a dysfunctional childhood often leads to spotty or nonexistent memories in adults. Though being raised by surrogate caretakers may not be painful per se, the experience is often devoid of any real meaning or substance. Therefore the memories of adult children of dysfunctional affluent families are frequently one-dimensional, lacking richness in their emotional texture—if they are present at all. For me, having only a few, shallow memories of my childhood leaves me feeling as though I never really had a childhood at all. I feel cheated, as though a large part of my life has been taken away or didn't exist at all. I'm never really sure whether the little pieces I do "remember" are from my own recollections or from something that someone has told me. Sometimes I feel that they really happened to someone else and that I was just watching.

Isolation may play a key role in this phenomenon. The lack of memory of childhood events, especially memories associated with inner landmarks, can result from the absence of an ongoing intimate familial exchange. In short, there is no one to help the child remember such events. In affluent homes with more than one child, the children's time may be so regulated that there is actually little interaction between siblings on a day-to-day basis. Instead, they will often attend different camps, boarding schools, or take individual lessons depending on the role for which they are slotted by such factors as gender and birth order. For an only child, of course, the isolation is even more complete. In either case, however, what is most lacking in the affluenza-afflicted home is the input of the parents in helping create a validating, authentic history for the family and the child. The relative absence of uncontrolled family leisure opportunities—whether around the dinner table, weekend camping, or long car trips together—precludes the sharing of memories and impressions that may influence or solidify later recollection.

Feelings of Failure: Depression and Anxiety

By the time I reached late adolescence, I had begun to use food, alcohol, and sex to help me fill the void left by my parents, hold fear at bay, and allow myself to almost believe that I felt as good about myself as everyone around me *seemed* to feel. Soon my addictions began to control my life. I began to use more food, more men, more drugs in a vain and seemingly endless attempt to make my life on the inside match the way it looked on the outside. After all, in the eyes of society, why shouldn't I be happy? I was the grand-daughter of Charles E. Wilson. My father was a handsome, successful businessman, known and respected throughout our small town of Delray Beach, Florida. My mother was a beautiful woman who frequently gave lavish parties for all her beautiful friends.

In spite of these outward trappings of happiness and comfort, I was filled with a growing, gnawing fear that if I stopped moving, achieving, performing, or laughing for one moment, everyone would find out that I was simply a fat, unlovable little girl whose own parents never cared enough for her to even eat dinner with her. With few healthy role models in my life, I learned as I went. I did what made me feel good at the moment—with an adolescent's reckless certainty that I would always be able to take care of myself in the face of danger.

In the light of my own experiences, I was not surprised to find during my research that the adolescent children of the rich and famous are more likely than other teenagers to abuse drugs and alcohol. David K. Wellisch, a psychologist who treats wealthy youngsters at the University of California at Los Angeles's Neuropsychiatric Institute, says that children of affluence generally suffer from a variety of developmental difficulties and deficits associated with their affluent lifestyles that make them highly anxious and unable to tolerate frustration.[8]

Alice Miller has also given us clues to the patterns of failure that are prevalent among the children and grandchildren of Family Founders. She contends that their high rates of suicide, extreme drug addiction, alcoholism, and other signs of a depressed personality are often the result of a narcissistically disturbed mother, a father who is physically and emotionally unavailable, unresolved abandonment issues, and the extreme pressure by the family and the public to conform and achieve.[9] These children are rarely encouraged to be themselves or to even find out who they might be. Being heirs to great fortunes and great names dictates the perimeters of their feelings and actions. Unlike their parents or grandparents, they receive little opportunity to choose or blaze their own path. Their families frequently determine their futures and enforce strong sanctions and rules to keep them within the acceptable boundaries. Financial persuasion and material gifts are held out as the carrots to entice them to follow a predetermined path.

Examples abound in the CEOs who carefully groom their sons to take over the family business, not necessarily because the heirs may find satisfaction in that particular line of work, but rather because the business is financially successful. The debutante parties, where the young women are "presented" to society, signify their readiness and supposed willingness to take their position in the upper echelons of the wealthy class. Subtly and not so subtly, these heirs are pushed, prodded, and polished in a very definite direction, often with many generations nodding in approval or disapproval as they grow and mature. Is it any wonder that many of them fail to live up to these overwhelming expectations? Combining their feelings of failure with the already present feelings of low self-esteem and self-worth usually results in intermittent, if not chronic, depression and anxiety.

Depression in particular has been a primary symptom of every affluent client whom I have treated. I have seen two basic components of depression in the majority of my clients and myself: anger turned inward and a loss of the self. These traits indicate that further emotional release work and more attention to self-care is needed. Depression will always occur when we deny our own emotional needs, feelings, and reactions.

Unrealistic Expectations and Lack of Accountability: The Perennial Child

Everyday problems are often accentuated in affluent dysfunctional families. Because children of affluence experience so little healthy frustration while living the "good life," they never develop the tolerance for frustration that is necessary to live a balanced, fulfilling life. When every material or experiential desire is satiated (especially via the proxy of a paid agent, servant, or nanny), the child does not learn to reign in or manage expectations. This is why in many ways, the child never grows up. The combination of immediate material gratification and consistent emotional deprivation and abandonment creates highly unrealistic expectations and needs in the adult. An adult-child of a dysfunctional affluent home seems destined to be disappointed and dissatisfied out in the "real" world where his or her demands and desires may not be met instantaneously or at all.

When they make serious mistakes, or when their addictions get them into trouble, wealthy people can almost always bail themselves out. If their money alone doesn't solve the problem, an expensive high-powered attorney usually can. So there is no price to pay for their errors, at least not immediately. This lack of accountability, however, strongly contributes to the illusion of perpetual adolescence, a false sense of entitlement, and the subsequent failure to mature emotionally and intellectually.[10] This hidden cost that affluent people pay with each unrectified mistake quietly contributes to their growing sense of worthlessness. When the "mistakes" become drug or alcohol addiction, the lack of accountability can be deadly. Furthermore, the longer the addict is protected from the consequences of his or her addiction, the harsher and more deadly those consequences become. For the rich, money can act as the codependent partner who protects the addict—to death. John Belushi, River Phoenix, and, recently, Margaux Hemingway are prime examples of this phenomenon.

Receiving Deferential Treatment

Children of affluence are frequently treated as very special people simply because they have money, a reason that has nothing to do with who they *really* are. This deferential treatment only adds to their feelings of low self-worth, because deep down these young people know that they have done nothing exceptional to deserve such treatment. Those who self-destruct or self-deny upon the inheritance of their "good" fortune, frequently believe at some level that they have not earned it. They realize that the person receiving all this attention is simply a hollow embodiment of the wealth and power that our culture has come to worship. In this knowledge lies the desperation that many of the wealthy come to feel. They know they have been raised to be frauds, and they have little or no sense of authentic identity or personal empowerment.

Within this realization, however, lie the tools for self-healing. If you are an affluent person, the first step to finding out who you really are is to confront and stop being who you *aren't*. For some young inheritors, this means leaving the family business or putting some psychological if not geographical distance between themselves and the powerful arm of their family. Nature abhors a vacuum and will certainly fill it—that is, direction will come if sought—but first one must create the opening. This is where a good therapist, preferably one schooled in the nuances of affluenza, can help effect positive and powerful change and growth. Helpful tools for healing and self-actualization will be discussed in detail in chapter 7.

Popular culture usually portrays these affluent young people as "spoiled" little rich kids, dilettantes, or the "idle" rich, feigning a superior, slightly bored air. They are believed to have little regard for the feelings of others, particularly their hired help, and are believed to hold an expectation that the rest of the world will recognize their social and financial prominence and bow down to them.

Although there may very well be some truth in the assumption that the affluent sometimes behave like pouty, willful children, the source of this behavior goes much deeper than simply wanting one's own way. The need to control the outcome of their lives, or anyone else's life, is always based on fear and lack of faith in themselves.

Issues of Self-worth and Identity: Did I Succeed or Did My Money Buy Success?

Contributing to their already low self-esteem is the fact that many wealthy people never have to prove themselves in the common market of the workplace. Because they have a shaky sense of self, they sometimes choose not to place themselves in a position to compare and contrast their abilities with those of their peers. They often create their own "jobs" or companies, or go into the family business, where the people around them are, in a sense, paid to approve of and compliment them. This atmosphere of false positive feedback reinforces the lessons of childhood with the nannies and nurses who were paid to cater to them. Thus begins the lifelong questioning: "Are these people being nice to me because they truly like me (respect me, love me, think I'm smart, and so on) or are they being nice to me because of my money?" The question comes in a thousand different forms, but it all boils down to issues of trust and self-confidence.

In order to resolve the mental and emotional stress of never knowing where they really stand, these young people begin to tell themselves that they really do somehow deserve to be treated differently. Not receiving accurate feedback for who they really are, they convince themselves that they must be the person others see them as being. Since others treat them with deference, they may begin to see themselves as more special and important. This can lead to the development of a narcissistic personality.

The "Silver-spoon" Syndrome

As mentioned earlier, this affluent type of narcissism has been aptly described as the "silver-spoon" syndrome by Joyce LeBeau. It is distinguished by a preoccupation with external appearances, little awareness of the inner self, and therefore an inability to nurture oneself or maintain psychological health.

LeBeau calls this syndrome "debilitating and pernicious, . . . characterized by a low sense of nurturance, depression, a high regard for public self, and a low regard for private self." Again, these traits result from "a strong preoccupation with social form" which leads many wealthy families to "consistently choose outward form over the child's legitimate emotional and developmental needs." The end result for the child is the creation of a "fork in growth patterns where the narcissistic pathology branches away from healthy ego development."

Silver-spoon children generally present in therapy without conscious awareness of having suffered any significant emotional trauma. But the presenting symptoms belie the child's own assessment, an assessment attributable more to low self-awareness than to an absence of real damage. Silver-spoon syndrome symptoms include "chronic mild depression, emptiness, boredom, . . . lack of empathy, high pursuit of pleasure, disinterest in work of any kind," and perhaps the most malignant of all, a pervasive belief that money will somehow fix everything.

These children are often worldly and arrogant on the one hand and simultaneously feel alienated and superfluous on the other. LeBeau recounts the story of "Arthur, just 18, graduated from high school with the highest SAT scores in his class" but who nonetheless somehow failed to be admitted into any college. "Despite a lavish lifestyle of private schools, wonderful vacations, computers, VCRs, a pool, cars—Arthur feels depressed, lonely, and undernurtured. He entertains grandiose notions of his ability and potential but falls short in reality because he has had no training, structure, or real guidance. Recently he had four car accidents, and after each one his parents immediately bought him a new car, no questions asked. They recognize that he is troubled but see no causative relationship to them or their lifestyle."[11]

Only years of hard work in a therapeutic setting is likely to ameliorate the psychological damage someone like Arthur received at a very young age from a lack of critical mirroring and nurturing experiences with his parents. In such cases, then, affluenza can be seen as directly causative of the silver-spoon syndrome, since money is the primary reason for the unavailability of the parents. One can readily understand why the syndrome is multigenerational. Should Arthur inherit his family fortune and start a family of his own, he will almost certainly be as absent for his children as his parents were for him.

What good has the family fortune really done a child like Arthur? Without extensive therapy or some kind of miracle, Arthur's life is destined to be one of unrelieved unhappiness. And all his family's money can do to help him, should he somehow muster the inner strength to seek his own healing, is to cover the psychotherapist's bills.

Trust and Fear:
Forming Intimate Relationships

We learn how to be good spouses, lovers, and companions by observing how our parents interact as we grow up. With absent parents, children of affluence often do not learn how to form and nurture intimate relationships. Even if their parents are present, the effects of affluenza may determine that neither the parent-child relationship nor the parent-parent relationship modeled for the child is particularly intimate or healthy. As we have seen, these children frequently form their primary relationship with a maid or servant. There is an unavoidable distance and inequality created by the power dynamics of the master-servant relationship. This becomes part of their distorted definition of intimacy and produces an assumption of control in future relationships that is extremely detrimental. As for parent to parent modeling, if the relationship is a positive one—that is, not characterized by chronic conflict and recrimination—then it is likely to be stylized and formal, to present an image of rigid control and restraint demanded by upper-class social mores. Even under the best of circumstances, then, intimacy appears as emotional distance and reserve. When feelings of abandonment combine with this lack of knowledge about intimacy, there is fertile soil for future dissatisfaction and repetitive patterns of unhealthy, short-term relationships.

Repeated bonding with parents or parent figures followed inevitably by the destruction of that bond produces a fear of abandonment that remains very much intact in many affluent adults. These adults either have a difficult time trusting in intimate relationships or are unable to trust at all. This is particularly true when the relationships are sexual. Quite simply, in a sexual relationship the potential for deep intimacy is greater, and therefore the risk of being hurt increases dramatically, making people with diminished ability to trust even more wary. They are inclined to reveal little of themselves in order to avoid the potential pain of abandonment. Yet it is only by revealing themselves and their fears that healing is possible.

This self-protection often involves hiding their wealth. Ironically, either divulging or hiding their financial status threatens the authenticity of the relationship. Concealing their wealth and the part it plays in their life decreases the chances for intimacy just as it decreases the level of honesty in the relationship. When, where, how, and how much to divulge are always tricky questions and can only be answered by each individual depending on the particular situation. Again, most people of affluence are wary, for they have frequently experienced a dramatic attitude change in others when their wealth is revealed. Some see the association with a wealthy person as potential for personal financial or status gain, whereas others perceive themselves below an affluent person in status and power, which makes both parties uncomfortable and impedes the development of intimacy.

While people often connect wealth with status and power, judging themselves "less than" a rich person, reverse snobbery is also possible, with the less-affluent person claiming moral or characterological superiority to the wealthy.

It is no wonder that adult children of dysfunctional affluent homes have a difficult time forming lasting intimate relationships of any kind. Not one of the wealthy people I interviewed has had even one lasting, successful relationship, although some are presently involved in relationships that seem to be working. One woman has never been in an intimate relationship, one woman never married but has had multiple partners, another woman has been married and divorced twice, and one young man married an older woman and is in the throes of reassessing his relationship.

I myself have been married and divorced twice and still struggle regularly with issues of trust.

Relationships:
Do They Love Me Because of Who I Am
or Because I'm Rich?

Most of the affluent people whom I've interviewed and all whom I've treated professionally report that they have a difficult time trusting the motives of their significant others. In addition to an intense fear of abandonment, an affluent individual is never quite sure why anyone is interested in forming a relationship with them. When there is more than one possible reason for a relationship to exist, it becomes more difficult to discern the true motivation.[12] People tend to choose the most obvious reason and look no further. For example, if a woman is very beautiful, many assume that her spouse has fallen in love with her because of her beauty, the most obvious, visible reason. Because of the powerful position of wealth in our culture, money becomes the defining quality of affluent people. It takes precedence over external beauty and most certainly over any internal beauty. Money therefore becomes the most obvious and powerful reason for the attraction. How many of us, seeing an attractive young woman with an unattractive or plain older man, have not thought, "Well, she must like him because of his money!"?

Because the affluent are often sought after and flattered by others, they develop a sense of insecurity about whether they are being accepted or pursued for themselves, or because of how much money they have. Driven to a defensive position by a world that by and large envies and resents them, they withdraw into fortresses, some figurative and some literal. Returning to the isolation of their childhood, many wealthy people become increasingly suspicious of the motives of others and let only a few trusted friends into their lives and homes. For some, it is only in their homes that they are truly themselves. There they can relax, often surrounded by heirlooms and family knickknacks that help define them as a person.

I am always hesitant and nervous when someone comes into my home for the first time. Because affluent people, myself included, often surround ourselves with our family's history, heirlooms may appear to be icons of wealth on display to impress visitors. In my home, there are many photographs of my family, particularly the Wilsons. I display awards, framed newspaper articles quoting my grandfather, political cartoons, photographs of my children on a succession of beautiful ponies and horses, and many antiques. To me, this is just family history, no different than the pictures on the piano or mantel in any home in America. But I know my possessions sometimes change the way people see and relate to me. To some, my money and social position suddenly become the main points of interest. I am no longer judged for who I am, what I believe in, what I stand for, and what I think. Their picture of me is seen through the lens of wealth. This lens frequently intimidates and distances people who are unaccustomed to such surroundings. It may impede or preclude the possibility of an equal, intimate friendship. Unconsciously, they may place me in an inaccessible place where they have never been before and so will not risk going. Most are either repelled by the money or drawn to it; few except other wealthy people are unaffected. I, like many rich people, have become increasingly proficient at sorting out those who value my friendship for the quality of the relationship and those who value the friendship for what they might gain, financially or socially.

When "Just" Succeeding Is Not Enough

In our culture, an individual's success is also relative to where he or she starts. People are perhaps rightfully perceived as a greater success when they go from "rags to riches" with no assistance. But, as we have seen, for children of affluence to succeed in their own eyes and the eyes of others, including their own families, they must *surpass* the previous generation. Maintaining the existing level of success or affluence is usually seen as failure in the golden ghetto. What might be considered a monumental success for a person of average means is merely the "expected" behavior for a second- or third-generation rich person. Ironically, if an affluent individual does manage to achieve a higher level of success, the outside world is likely to believe that this success was somehow "bought," not earned. During my interview with Julilly Kohler, she recounted her first vivid, painful memory of having an accomplishment discounted because of her famous name and how much money her family had.

> One afternoon in kindergarten, two girls and I were talking and one girl said, "What's three plus three?" and I said, "That's six." And then I said, "What's one hundred plus one hundred?" The other girls didn't know and I said, "Well, that's two hundred." One of the girls turned to me and said, "You know that because you live in a big house and you're rich." I was just dumbstruck. As if they would think that had anything to do with it. I realized that there was nothing I could say to change that. . . . I was just totally incapacitated. I remember the feeling of standing there as if I were enclosed in a column and I couldn't even raise my hand to do anything about it. All my energy was taken away. So I just stood there. Then they turned and laughed and ran away. I stood there for about five minutes not knowing what to do.

Such experiences, repeated over the course of a lifetime, often lead affluent people who are successful to doubt the legitimacy of their abilities and talents. They may experience conflicting emotions about their accomplishments, uncertain that they deserve the success that does come their way. They may feel pressure to try even harder and harder to somehow prove that they have succeeded in their own right. The late James Merrill, an accomplished and well-known poet who was also the son of Charles Merrill of Merrill Lynch, said, "People thought I must have paid to get my poems published, which used to bother me. I suppose I was eager to achieve something of my own, but I don't worry about that anymore." Because of his inheritance, James was able to pursue his art full time, unlike most poets. He was aware of the chasm that this created: "I felt that in a way I was set apart from [struggling writers] and that therefore I had to try even a bit harder than they were trying to prove myself. It's possible also that people might not take me seriously—just the way I myself don't take rich people seriously because I have a feeling they're out of touch with reality."[13]

Being successful in one's chosen career is, for most people, an esteem-building, gratifying experience. For the wealthy, it can become lost and devoid of meaning because of how other people, including other rich people, view the accomplishment. This can result in low self-worth and a lack of self-confidence that no amount of money can correct.

What Is the Right Kind of "Support" for Your Children?

On the other hand, for those able to rise to the occasion, the wealthy parent might be an extremely positive role model for future motivation. Peter Buffet not only doesn't mind that his father, Warren Buffet, intends to leave him very little upon his death, he looks forward to making his own billions. To Peter, this seems a realistic and attainable goal. He did, however, inherit two thousand dollars from his grandfather, Congressman Howard Buffet. His father invested that money in his company, Berkshire-Hathaway, until Peter came of age. Due to the incredible success of Berkshire,

Peter's investment earned him half a million dollars. Peter used this "nest egg" to buy sound equipment to start a successful career in music. To his father's credit, he encouraged Peter to venture forth on his own. With his dad's emotional support and encouragement, Peter was able to feel good enough about himself and his abilities to follow his heart and succeed.

Warren Buffet is obviously aware of the immense price his son would pay in terms of self-esteem, self-confidence, and motivation if financial success were simply handed to him. Unfortunately, in my research I have found few parents with that much flexibility and foresight. Usually, the workaholic Family Founder has an inordinately high need to control his environment, compulsively manipulating his children's lives and careers in the bargain.

James Merrill, mentioned above, is another example of a child who successfully avoided the entrapments of wealth. James's love was literature and he began to write poetry at an early age. When his college professors encouraged him to pursue a career in poetry, his father not only showed an interest in his writing, but suggested that his son "go about it in the most serious way possible."[14] Although his father paid to publish his son's first book of poetry, James soon became an acclaimed poet in his own right.

James Merrill and Peter Buffet have two very important things in common that contributed to their personal success: (1) At crucial times in their emotional and career development, they were supported and encouraged by their fathers to make their own choices and take risks; (2) they chose artistic careers that require talent—something money can't buy. When I asked Peter if he ever wondered if he could have made it completely on his own, without the original bequest from his grandfather, he admitted to some original guilt around the inheritance. He claimed, however, that his guilt disappeared when it was obvious that his success was based on his talent. Until the extraordinary success of his work on the sound track for *Dances with Wolves,* he says that he entertained some lingering doubts, a problem that a large number of children from affluent families never overcome.

Peter has not, however, totally escaped the negative repercussions of being born into an affluent family. His father was a workaholic and Peter has experienced the emotional deprivation that occurs when a parent is absent much of the time. He lacked the concrete interaction with an accessible role model that is critical for healthy psychological development. Because of this, he feels that his self-confidence and self-esteem have suffered. As he has become more successful and affluent, he finds himself less trusting of others' motivations in relationships. However, he sees these insecurities fading with his increasing ability to successfully meet new challenges and take risks.

My friend Robin Kyle, the daughter of a wealthy financier, has both wealth and artistic talent. Robin, however, has not yet been able to achieve consistent success in her chosen career. Because of incessant criticism from her domineering father, she closed her art studio and withdrew from public scrutiny. Many children of affluence have little patience or ability to stay on task in the face of frustration and less-than-immediate gratification. Without the self-esteem that encouraging parents help generate, Robin and many like her struggle to sustain motivation. In careers as well as in intimate relationships, when the going gets rough, people with affluenza tend to move on to a different career or another person. A large part of our healing process involves learning to discern the difference between running away and appropriately choosing a different direction.

John Sedgwick, the author of *Rich Kids,* admits that although he liked the individuals he interviewed, he admired only a few — the ones who had accomplished something with their money. Although the affluent young men and women he wrote about came into their wealth by birth, they had to do something more, achieve something more, contribute something more to prove that they deserved what they had and that they were indeed "successful." Spending money freely for one's own fun and enjoyment did not qualify in anyone's mind, including those he interviewed, as a responsible way to handle wealth. Unlike money earned by a Family Founder or any other financially ambitious person, inherited wealth takes on a life and personality of its own. It demands to be treated in a certain way. It comes with a heavy price tag of responsibility.

Free-fall without a Parachute

I remember with clarity and grief the feeling following my mother's death in 1978 when I inherited the bulk of my wealth. It was as if I had suddenly been pushed from a plane with a parachute that wouldn't open. I felt a sudden withdrawal of all the parameters that defined my day-to-day behavior. When you inherit money, your relationships change in threatening and confusing ways. The balance of power within marriages and friendships shifts perceptively. Often "groupies" suddenly appear, eager to spend your money for you. You need no longer work for survival, a primary daily motivator. Within that huge block of suddenly available time, the choices and options for behavior are endless and often terrifying. Remember, this occurs at a time when you are experiencing grief and loss over the death of a parent or other close relative. Is it any wonder that the "choices" individuals make at a time like that are rarely healthy, responsible, or productive? Only a small percentage of the children of the affluent seem able to find the emergency cord on that parachute before they hit the ground.

Though sudden success or inherited wealth would seem like a blessing, that is seldom the case. A study done on lottery winners found that the more money an individual won, the more self-gratification and permissiveness entered his or her life, and the lower future motivation and aspirations became.[15] Self-gratification and permissiveness translate into many psychopathologies, most notably the excessive substance abuse found among the affluent. Since the majority of people in our culture see the accumulation of wealth as their primary life goal, lottery winners feel as if they have now "made it" and see no reason to strive for further personal or professional growth or success. In many cases of sudden or inherited wealth, the very strength of the gift seems to diminish the strength of the receiver, the opposite of the intended effect. For example, Peter Buffet is convinced that he would not work nearly as hard as he does, nor be as successful, if he were assured of inheriting his father's money.

Although the challenges are many, I feel great hope for this generation of "children" of affluence. I think there is a rapidly growing awareness that just as their money solves many problems, so it creates its own. Pain is a great motivator. When the fire gets hot enough, we move. Many of us have found a saner, healthier way—walking a path that heals the wounds of our pasts. Most of us have children and would do anything we could to ensure that their lives are better, happier, more joyful and serene than ours have been. I believe in the ability of this generation of children to open their eyes and choose a different way. It has happened before; indeed, much family wealth began with people of intelligence and motivation. Along with each individual's unique strengths and gifts, the genetic heritage is available as a positive resource for those who choose to use it constructively.

NOTES

1. Malcom Forbes and Jeff Bloch, *What Happened to Their Kids?: Children of the Rich and Famous* (New York: Simon and Schuster, 1990), 114.
2. Julilly Kohler, interview by author, September 1995.
3. U.S. Department of Health and Human Services. National Center for

Health Statistics. *Annual Summary of Births, Marriages, Divorces, and Deaths: United States,* 1994, 43, no. 13 (23 October 1995).

4. Joyce LeBeau, "The 'Silver-Spoon Syndrome' in the Super Rich: The Pathological Linkage of Affluence and Narcissism in Family Systems," *American Journal of Psychotherapy* 42 (1988): 426–36.

5. P. Edidin, "Drowning in Wealth," *Psychology Today,* April 1989, 34.

6. Alice Miller, *The Drama of the Gifted Child: The Search for the True Self,* trans. Ruth Ward (New York: Basic Books, 1981), 47.

7. Jeffrey M. Masson, *The Assault on Truth: Freud's Suppression of the Seduction Theory* (New York: Harper Collins), quoted in Gloria Steinem, "The Trouble with Rich Women," *Ms.,* June 1986, 43.

8. M. Norman, "Growing Up Fast: Problems in the Fast Lane," *Psychology Today,* December 1984, 70.

9. Miller, *The Drama of the Gifted Child,* 34–48.

10. A. Toufexis, "The Woes of Being Wealthy," *Time,* 9 (February 1988): 95.

11. LeBeau, "The 'Silver-Spoon Syndrome' in the Super Rich," 428–29.

12. Steven Berglas, *The Success Syndrome: Hitting Bottom When You Reach the Top* (New York: Plenum Press, 1986), 86.

13. Ibid, 175.

14. Forbes and Bloch, *What Happened to Their Kids?,* 175.

15. M. Abrahamson, "Sudden Wealth, Gratification and Attainment: Durkheim's Anomie of Affluence Reconsidered," *American Sociological Review* 45, no. 2 (1980): 49–57.

5

THE COCKTAIL PARTY: MONEY, GENDER, AND POWER

Girls from monied families, of course, are expected to marry men of similar or greater wealth. If their fathers own businesses and there is no male heir, a son-in-law may be groomed to take over before a daughter is considered, quite apart from the skills of either. Gender speaks louder than intelligence, experience, even interest in or aptitude for the work involved.

MARGARET RANDALL
The Price You Pay

IN SPITE OF THIRTY YEARS OF MODERN FEMINISM and more than a decade of the men's movement, men and women still have many unresolved issues surrounding money, power, work, and intimacy. These differences are clearly evident in the corporate arena where the reins of power are still jealously guarded by men. Money and power have traditionally had such a masculine aura that it is almost considered unfeminine for women to attempt to scale the heights of big business.

These attitudes can be observed in the dynamics at just about any upscale social function. Here men cluster together discussing business, money, and power. The very way they talk denotes their pecking order. In no time at all, a group of men will establish who is the most successful, powerful, and affluent—often one and the same person. Among men, participating in this kind of conversation is acceptable, expected, even respected behavior. Should the same conversation emanate from a group of women, however, it would be considered "unseemly," embarrassing, and boastful. Others at the function would be uncomfortable with this group of women, possibly even avoiding them.

I'd like to think that not all who attend these society functions are so narrow-minded, but in my experience most people continue to be so. In many academic, artistic, and cultural gatherings throughout the world, I do believe that men and women meet as equals without regard to financial position. In high-society America, however, it is simply not the way the social system functions, at least not yet. Even though many women have become entrepreneurs in recent years, only a handful have achieved the status of CEOs at Fortune Five Hundred companies. I found no women among the Family Founders in my research.

The Pendulum Swings

Although we are *beginning* to treat men and women with greater equality within the workplace, we are also acknowledging just how much the two sexes are different. Much has been written about male and female management styles; for example, male managers generally like to operate within hierarchical structures while most women enjoy more equal, give-and-take interactions within their teams.

Because we are in a time of great transition and growth in our culture, it is also a time of great confusion. In order for change to occur, the pendulum must swing from one extreme or the other before people will sit up and take notice. Human beings usually only change when they get uncomfortable enough, and extremes help us pay attention because they cause concern or discomfort.

A good example of this "when-the-fire-gets-hot-enough" phenomenon is the women's movement. In order for men, and in many cases, other women, to take notice of the problems surrounding women's lives, it was necessary for some women to take their demands and their behaviors to great extremes. Bra burning may seem silly and bizarre in the nineties, but it sure garnered attention for the movement in the sixties. Sexual harassment lawsuits over nude workplace pinups may seem frivolous to some, but they convey a profound message about how women want to be regarded and what they think is fair. Such tactics produce great discomfort, great resistance, and great change in the way women are treated in our country today. For many people, women *and* men, modern feminism was the wake-up call that provoked a much-needed shift in attitudes toward women in general.

Unfortunately, it is the individual men and women of this century who have been caught up in these changes and have had to deal with them. The socialization we grew up with—what our parents modeled for us as the "right" behavior—and the kinds of behaviors we now profess to believe in, are frequently very different. We find ourselves in a state of dissonance, where our insides and our outsides are at bitter odds with one another. For example, although we say it is just as acceptable for young men to marry older women as it is for young women to marry older men, in reality, the latter is much more acceptable. Likewise, although we say we are comfortable with a woman who has a great deal of wealth or power, in truth it makes us feel uneasy.

Another way of looking at the mixed cultural messages we must live with is covert versus overt beliefs. A *covert belief* is defined as one that we have internalized over the years in a variety of ways—through our parents, friends or societal beliefs; the media, the church, government, and so on. Throughout every day, through every sense we have, we are taking in information about how we should act and think, processing it, saving it, and filing it away for future reference. In many ways, our covert beliefs are a product of emotional responses to people and situations, and often assimilate unconsciously. Our *overt beliefs,* on the other hand, come from a more conscious, intellectual, cognitive place. Overt beliefs are those we frequently *decide* to believe in, because we think they are right or good. They represent what we *say* we believe—the face that we show to the world—and reflect how we think we *should* feel.

Regardless of the intellectual gymnastics our generation has gone through to change our belief systems, to a large extent we have internalized what our parents modeled and what others around us seem to believe in. As often as we say we don't care what other people think, the truth is that we *do* care about the opinions and judgments of our peers, our families, and our communities. And this is why our perception of their opinions and judgments often become our own.

Financial Disparity

There is no arena where the inequality between the sexes is more evident than in the world of money. The more wealth someone has, the greater the possibility of disagreement and inequity at many levels within the power dynamics of the relationship. This is particularly true in intimate relationships. Time and again, in my own life and in the lives of my clients and friends, I have seen how difficult it is for even the most self-assured man to deal with a partner who has considerably more money than he has. In a society where men have traditionally held the role of primary breadwinner and provider, time-honored roles run deep and are hard to give up or change. Men customarily define success and find their self-esteem and identity within the confines of their career and how much money they make. Because our society continues to intertwine success, money, and power, when a man becomes intimate with a very wealthy woman, his covert beliefs about role and power are often called into question. He is unconsciously asked to find balance in the relationship while employing something other than the usual scale of measurement. When a woman has or earns more money than her husband or lover, it can create for him (and for her) an inner discordance that can ultimately be fatal to the relationship.

For women, particularly those who consider themselves proponents of equality, it is problematic accepting the difficulties of forging healthy relationships with men who have less money than they do. I have been in many relationships in which I tried to encourage interpersonal dynamics based on the assumption that it didn't matter if a man had a more modest income than I did. Why should it matter where or who the money came from as long as we were emotionally and physically happy with one another? The sad truth is that, because of deeply internalized socialization, it usually *does* matter. Because we live in a culture that equates money with power and control, and socializes men to need both to function as respected individuals, being in a relationship with a wealthy woman puts many men into a situation they are ill-equipped to handle. The man who is psychologically capable of handling such a relationship may find himself belittled and discounted by his peers. The situation also proves awkward for women who are socialized to believe that men will take care of their needs, including their financial security. As a result, many women of wealth find themselves drawn only to men of equal or greater wealth, unable to look beyond such a limited measure of character and compatibility.

"Marrying Money": The Gigolo vs. True Love

Creating and sustaining a healthy intimate relationship is difficult for everyone, but it is even more complicated for a person who is wealthy. Meeting potential partners is often challenging and some-times even terrifying. As we have seen, money is a powerful attrac-tor, and affluent people must be on the lookout for those who are interested not in them, but in their real or perceived bank ac-counts. Years of dealing with potential fortune hunters often makes affluent people extremely cautious about protecting themselves and their hearts. The need to be discerning creates a level of mis-trust in any new relationship that remains until it is either proved or disproved. Again, this mistrust is exacerbated by money.

We can see in this a double standard. When a man is contem-plating an intimate relationship with a woman, it would be con-sidered both rude and inappropriate for him to show an interest in her finances, particularly if she is rich and he isn't. On the other hand, it is somewhat acceptable in our culture for a woman to show interest in a man's financial status and allow his income to influence her decision of whether to spend more time with him. In our patriarchal society, hardly an eyebrow is raised when a wealthy man marries a woman of average means. The traditional male power structure remains intact, and the wealth flows in the acceptable, conventional direction—from the man to the woman. When a financially successful or wealthy woman marries a man of average means, however, people are all too quick to assume that he has a "gigolo" arrangement.

Women in our culture are generally expected and encouraged to choose partners who are wealthier than they are. This is especially true among the affluent. When a woman of inherited wealth marries a man of modest means, she is believed to have married "beneath" herself, out of desperation or the inability to "catch" anyone in her own social world. Many of her peers lose respect for her, assuming that her partner has "married money," and that somehow she is not bright enough to ascertain his motives.

For the honest, hard-working nonaffluent man who marries a rich woman for love, these cultural assumptions can sorely undermine his self-esteem; he may eventually begin to question his own motives for entering the relationship. At the very least, it creates an obstacle that is not present in a relationship between partners of equal wealth. As I look back on the dynamics of the relationship between my mother and my father, I am convinced that my mother's generous act of lending my father money to start his car dealership contributed to the process of disempowerment that led to his steady downhill slide into inactivity and alcoholism.

A "gift" between wife and husband carries implications similar to the gift of inheritance bestowed upon a male heir. Unlike their female counterparts who inherit wealth, men consciously and unconsciously expect themselves—as others expect them—to be the primary provider in the family structure. After all, in our society supplying money within a relationship is still the most acknowledged form of "providing." (This custom, by the way, minimizes or completely discounts non-income-related contributions to the family such as child-nurturance and household management, traditionally the venue of women, at least in nonaffluent homes. Again, an over-emphasis on the value of money as a goal in and of itself—as *the* goal, in fact—skews reality, in this case the perception of real value in a home economy.) By receiving money from another source, such as his wife or an inheritance, a man's self-image *as a man* and the image he displays to others is called into question. In the words of a woman married to a man with inherited wealth, "It emasculated Don to inherit the family money." Not only does it call into question his ability to provide for his family, but it also undermines his need-driven motivation to test his range of other abilities. He loses the power to separate out what has been given to him and what is uniquely his.

On the other hand, the poor or middle-class woman whom the rich man marries is often young and beautiful, a "trophy wife," frequently a second or third version of his first wife. In the macho world of big business, she is not a threat to the power structure and is perceived by his cronies as harmless at worst and an attractive asset at best. No one cares whether she's after his money because it's assumed that he can take care of himself, unlike his "gullible" female counterpart. Also, the rich man who marries or dates a woman of average means because he truly loves her does not face the array of obstacles that are present when the woman is rich and the man is not.

For the woman whose income is or becomes greater than her partner's, these underlying cultural beliefs often begin to eat away at the very foundation of their relationship. Without a conscious awareness of how the dysfunctions of affluenza disrupt lives, without either self-help or therapeutic intervention, these men and women are doomed to feel the strain and disruption these unfair sex-role stereotypes can cause for their relationship.

Sex-Role Stereotypes

As we have seen, from birth we are all bombarded with subtle and not-so-subtle messages that strongly influence who we are, what we believe, and what we do with our lives. The most basic of these messages is that men should have more power than women. How women with money (read: power) are commonly viewed is evidenced by the quip that "a man who marries a rich woman earns every penny he gets out of it." To a large extent, this is because many men judge their status and self-worth by how much money/power they have.

Unfortunately, this is not only true of men. The fortune of a plain or even unattractive man can be a powerful aphrodisiac for many women. For women, however, their most valuable asset is still that ever-so-vulnerable and illusive attribute, sexual attractiveness. If anyone doubts this, they have only to look at the multi-billion-dollar fashion and cosmetic industries, the millions spent on plastic surgeries in this country every year, the cultural obsession with staying young, and the preternaturally perfect female images screaming from the pages of hundreds of women's magazines. The cultural imperative to be beautiful translates directly and tragically into the world of the affluent and is further accentuated by the presence of money, power, and control. If a rich man's wife is no longer young and attractive, he can—and often does—trade her in for a new model.

Many of the middle- and upper-middle class women of today are encouraged to have careers—to do more with their lives, their intelligence, and their talent than their mothers did. On the other hand, women who inherit wealth or are married to wealthy men are not expected to work and, if they do, their careers are often regarded by others as mere hobbies. When Jackie Kennedy Onassis went to work as an editor at Doubleday, she was instantly regarded by the press and popular media as a dilettante. No amount of protest from her superiors could quell that widespread belief, however unfair it was.

In other ways, however, the cultural pressure to achieve is even greater than it was before. The success of a rich man or woman is no longer defined, as it once was, by the level of the individual's social acceptance. It is no longer sufficient to merely have the money and live a life of leisure. Men in particular must continue to cultivate their wealth in a manner that makes it clear that they are educated about and involved in the process of *making* money. As their financial worth increases, so does our cultural regard and esteem for them. Although the affluent give lip service to admiring and supporting a wealthy woman on the same track, in reality, her social world finds ways to quietly pull her back down to where they believe she belongs—in the home or at the charity function.

In many ways it is easier for a woman of average means to climb the corporate ladder, since it is understood and accepted in today's world that many women must fend for themselves. We still believe it would be "better," however, if she could find some nice man to care for her financially. Simply reverse the gender roles and we immediately see how stereotypical and far from equal our belief systems truly are.

In the world of affluence, gender roles are even more clearly defined. As children, young male heirs are expected to excel in scholastic subjects, such as math and science, that will ensure their ability to carry on the family fortune. Young female heirs are encouraged to concentrate on those talents that will bring about their marriage to a suitable partner, someone in their own class who is at least their financial equal and who has the ability to manage their finances for them. Wealthy girls are taught to look good and to be talented and gracious hostesses. Any musical or artistic talent they might display is met with great approval. Should they fall a little short in the sciences, no one really cares. It's assumed they will never need those skills, and it's even a little embarrassing if they show a desire to learn them. In some particularly archaic circles of wealth, knowing about business or science is actively discouraged. After all, it might not be acceptable for a young woman to know more than her future husband in the male-dominated financial arena.

The consequences of this socialization are appalling. I believe that many affluent women unconsciously choose a less financially successful route to ensure that their odds remain favorable in the relationship arena. Women with inherited wealth may downplay their financial acumen in an attempt to appear less powerful to prospective partners.

In a better world, a *new* American dream, men and women would glean their power not from outside themselves but from the vast store of resources within. In the long run, our only true power comes from knowing ourselves, speaking our truth in all relationships, acknowledging our feelings, and taking responsibility for our actions and letting others do the same. To diminish ourselves for another's approval effectively kills off a part of the self and makes what we have to offer less than whole. When people enter a relationship expecting the other person to supply some missing part of themselves, the relationship is doomed to be a failure at worst and a great struggle at best.

Money as a Taboo Subject

Since money and personal power are so closely wed in our culture, money has become a very difficult subject to discuss. Most adults simply avoid talking about the amount of money they have or don't have, as it makes them feel weak and vulnerable. We fear that information will be used against us somehow, and we know that there is always someone with more money and power than we have. Because we have made money a banner defining our worth, we are careful to protect our assets from any close scrutiny lest the fabric of the banner begins to fray. If we have based our entire sense of identity and empowerment on the amount of money we have, then we better make very certain that our power source remains hidden and protected. This is especially important if the show of wealth is more smoke and mirrors than real net worth. In these days of seemingly endless credit, it is fairly easy to appear a great deal wealthier than you are.

There are some definite class and gender differences contained within this unspoken rule. Wealthy men live and work in an arena that makes it both acceptable and expedient to discuss their finances, if not their net worth. For women in the same circles it would be "unladylike" to discuss theirs; it's just there. Joking with one young female heir who was hesitant to talk about the value of the jewelry she wore, John Sedgwick suggested that they discuss her sex life instead. Much to his surprise, she was more willing to talk about that. "That would be much easier," she replied airily. "It's so vulgar to talk about how much things cost."[1] Sex, unlike wealth, is something that almost everyone has at one time or another. It is a common denominator. Another young wealthy woman became a counselor at a center specializing in the treatment of rape victims. Although she could get up in front of large crowds and frankly discuss the unfair prejudice and treatment of those who are raped, she was unable to bring herself to open up about her wealth.

Trophy Wives:
Low Self-esteem, Low Self-worth, and High Dependency

During her travels throughout the country in the seventies and eighties to speak to women, Gloria Steinem began to empathize more and more with the wealthy women she encountered. These wives of powerful, affluent men, even when wealthy in their own right, had no work of their own and identified most strongly with two other groups: prostitutes and domestics. In a glorified, socially approved way, that was the work they felt they were doing. Their self-esteem was as low as that of the women in those two professions. Since it was sometimes harder for them to change "employers" than it was for prostitutes and domestics, their sense of dependency was painfully high. Steinem could always discern the status of the women at these meetings by their age, because the older wives frequently had been "traded in" for new ones (trophy wives). If the business that was the primary source of wealth was in the wife's family, the marriage lasted longer. The husband would be more likely to wait until the father-in-law died and then leave his wife when the will could not be changed. Even after the divorce, the ex-husband was still more likely to control the family business. If a woman got divorced from a man who had less money, or who didn't keep the business, he would probably get a settlement or an unconditional lump sum, unlike alimony payments given to ex-wives.[2]

Returning to visit her high school friends and then later the well-to-do alumni at her Smith College twenty-fifth reunion, Steinem found the contrast between the two groups of classmates startling. The women from her high school class, through necessity, had become self-sufficient and self-confident. Of the Smith College women, Steinem writes: "Some of the most privileged were self-deprecating, lost, and fearful of losing their looks or their husbands. They might be taking courses or acquiring advanced degrees, but more as an end than a means. Generally, they seemed uncertain that they could be independent, much less have an impact on the world."[3]

Rich women do not need to work for financial survival, the most common reason for anybody's discovery of their capabilities. Often, they do not even have the responsibility of managing the family portfolio. If she does work, the rich woman is often resented by her co-workers or forced to hide her true situation. She knows that what she is likely to earn is a mere pittance compared to the family income. The deepest reason for the self-deprecation and uncertainty of rich women may be the simple fact that, "The closer we are to power, the more passive we must be kept. Intimacy and access make rebellion very dangerous."[4]

When a woman earns a great deal of money or inherits wealth, she also acquires power. Because our culture has defined power in a very masculine sense, when a woman becomes financially successful she may at the same time become less successful socially. If she is not already uncomfortable in her own skin with this new "masculine" aura, she is frequently made to feel uncomfortable by her male cohorts who are threatened by her success. Unable to compete financially, they may find ways to "bring her down to size," emotionally or socially, through undermining actions and remarks. Interestingly, sexual harassment of women within certain fields has little to do with actual sex and much more with scaring the women off the male turf, in essence a power struggle. This is particularly true within traditionally male professions such as fire-fighting, construction, and investment banking.

The insidious belief that power is somehow unfeminine undermines the self-confidence and self-esteem of every woman in our country today, rich or poor. Because women define themselves by their relationships to a far greater extent than men do, we are consciously and unconsciously hesitant to do anything that might jeopardize an existing or potentially intimate connection. Since power is traditionally bound to males, we frequently take a step back in our pursuit of or management of money, innately knowing that to hold such power may damage our relationships. In our dysfunctional society a "balanced" relationship is one in which the money and power are traditionally far from balanced. "A pedestal is as much a prison as any other small space."[5]

Men, in general, are not so dependent on love relationships for their sense of self as women are, in large part because the culture offers men many more alternatives. The high self-esteem and sense of power that men derive from financial success makes it less likely that they will feel threatened by a woman who might be interested in them for their money. Furthermore, men who inherit money seem somewhat more comfortable with assuming the family heritage and wealth as their own than do women. Steinem notes that women of wealth who choose to rebel against the traditional family roles often do so in a "traditionally feminine way: they punish themselves."[6] Most eventually conform and marry the expected wealthy consort. The sons are expected to take over the family business. Young women with no brothers, as was my case, are encouraged to bring home sons-in-law who will perpetuate the family dynasty.

The part that money plays takes on an even greater significance when any woman or man contemplates a long-term relationship. As mentioned earlier, a financially successful man is often more attractive to any woman, rich or poor. A wealthy or ambitious woman who makes a lot of money may initially *appear* more attractive to a man, but, in reality, caution sets in when a man begins to wonder if it is really desirable to deviate from traditional power roles.

Increased Incidence of Incest with Increased Wealth

Steinem makes an interesting, if unproven proposition about incest among the wealthy. She contends that sexual abuse of little girls by men in their households increases with the dependency of the women and children and the contrasting power of the man. As a man's financial worth increases, so does his perceived power and his sense of ownership of women—a *noblesse oblige* among men, if you will. Add to that society's reluctance to intervene on behalf of children who may have been sexually abused, and there is ample reason to suspect a higher incidence of incest inside powerful affluent families than is found in nonaffluent families. Certainly, there is more reluctance within the legal system to punish those at fault when they are surrounded by the increased protection of wealth.[7]

Domestic violence, once assumed to be the province of the

poor, is now known to exist at every income level. Although wealth better enables a battered woman to find safety for herself and her children, pressure against bringing legal charges, and the husband's ability to legally defend himself also increases as social status goes up.[8]

Money and Women's Pain

Because of the veiled and sometimes outright resentment and hostility that some nonaffluent women feel toward their rich counterparts, there has been little support for affluent women within the feminist movement. (Outside the feminist movement, ambitious women are similarly disparaged.) The obvious differences between these two groups make it difficult for them to find common ground. Other effects of affluence make the division even more apparent and awkward. Steinem noted that the rich women she went to college with at Smith "seemed a little apologetic for having a 'daddy-ship' instead of a scholarship"; for having money they didn't earn or control; for a lifestyle they were likely to continue through marriage to someone as affluent as themselves; and generally for carrying something as unfeminine as power, if one equates power and money. The following quote exemplifies how rich women were subtly excluded from the women's movement in the seventies:

> If you've grown up in a house so ramshackle and unheated that you're ashamed to invite your friends over, it takes a while to understand that your privileged friends may be ashamed to invite you home for the opposite reason. . . . We talked about child care in ways that excluded women who had maids and thus no confidence they could even run their own houses, or about reproductive rights even if that meant disparaging women who could pay for illegal abortions but risked their safety nonetheless. . . .[9]

As recounted in the introduction, in the spring of 1966 I became pregnant by my first boyfriend; I was sixteen years old. We were both from dysfunctional, noncommunicative, affluent families and neither one of us had been told the "facts of life." Over a two-year period and with great tenderness, we taught one another to love. The result was as predictable as it was horrifying to both of our rich, proper families. After a painful, embarrassing meeting of the two families, I was swept away to New York for what was then a very illegal and very expensive abortion. We stayed in our usual corner suite at the Plaza. I was drugged, taken to Newark in a limousine, and awoke safely tucked back in my bed at the hotel. I remember nothing of the operation itself. The subject was never mentioned again and it was many years before my parents trusted me again with men. The psychological implications for me were quickly swept under the rug with the rest of the incident.

Our money had allowed my parents to buy their way out of my "mistake." However, it would be very wrong to assume that there were, therefore, no consequences. Because of the swift and efficient handling of the problem, it quickly took on the same surreal quality as the rest of my childhood. The feelings were denied, rapidly and neatly suppressed, and it was several years before the reality of what had happened began to surface. Sitting safely at lunch one day years later, a friend began to discuss abortion. I became nauseous and passed out cold. Unable to express my feelings verbally because I was consciously unaware of the repressed experience, my body nonetheless responded to the personal horror I subconsciously associated with the conversation. Somewhere deep inside me was the unexpressed rage, pain, and fear of a wounded young woman. In addition to providing an abortion as safe as money could buy at that time, that same money helped further bury the wound.

Lack of Trust

As explored in chapter 4, the issue of trust, paramount in every emotional connection, becomes magnified in an intimate relationship that involves a lot of money. When seeking an honest, intimate relationship, women and men of wealth or financial prowess must carefully weigh whether their prospective partner is in the relationship for the money or for them.

Although it is easy in our culture to become over-identified with one's money and success, the truth is, a person's financial worth is only a part of who they are, not the whole. Our culture has encouraged us to trust only what we can see and touch, material things, things that are attained only with money. What is the way out of this dilemma? Although we must learn to trust our judgment, our intelligence, our instincts, and our feelings when it comes to discerning a person's motives, the real ability to trust and be vulnerable to another must come from a higher place that has nothing whatsoever to do with money. Ultimately, letting go, trusting, and putting ourselves into the hands of a higher power clarifies the issues around relationships and trust. Due to fear, it is not easy to let go of our need to try to control the outcome of any given situation. If we can turn things over to a power greater than ourselves, however, we will often find that the issue of whether or not to trust another person takes care of itself.

Wealthy women seem to have an especially difficult time finding balance and trust in an intimate relationship. As we have seen, rather than being an asset, a woman's money tends to be an impediment to love.[10] My research, as well as that of others, indicates that it is preferable for wealthy women in particular to find partners of equal or greater financial worth. Yet most of the young affluent people in Sedgwick's *Rich Kids*, and all of the people whom I interviewed—both men and women—have chosen spouses whose finances were not equal to their own. This is due to a combination of things: practicality and availability, the decline of high-society festivities, and a desire by the children of the sixties and seventies to be "normal," to fit into the mainstream.[11] Since finding a spouse is often a long and arduous process for the wealthy, many wealthy women are slow to leave even highly unsatisfactory relationships. They often feel, at some fundamental level, that men are repelled by their money; they fear that the relationships may be very difficult to replace.

Women Are *Good Money Managers*

Stereotypes concerning women and money abound in our culture. Women are often portrayed, especially by the media, as compulsive shoppers who are severely lacking in any sort of financial comprehension. But it is a false assumption that women are poor money managers. A 1984 study of this belief, referred to as the "merry-widow" syndrome, found little evidence of the dissipation of wealth by women after the death of their spouses. In general, well-to-do widows tend to preserve and often increase their wealth during the years of widowhood.[12] This information is particularly interesting considering the fact that people who come into sudden wealth, such as those who win the lottery or inherit an unsuspected fortune, show a greater tendency to spend their money in permissive self-gratification and frequently suffer a loss of ambition and future aspirations. It would follow that the sudden death of a spouse and greater access to large sums of money might have the same effect upon the widows.

I attribute the fact that these women *do not* run out and squander their fortunes to both their familiarity with handling affluence over time and the greater maturity of age. Many widows may also have achieved equal access to the money before their husbands died. Unlike young recipients of inherited wealth, they seem to be able to handle the money in responsible, constructive ways, in spite of the fact that they are dealing with grief and loss.

Although women are relatively new to the world of big business, there is some indication that they might actually be more frugal than their male counterparts. Anxious to excel and determined to be successful in this male-dominated world, they are cautious with their resources and more reluctant to take outrageous risks that might lead to financial failure—since it is often assumed that they *will* fail. Failure can therefore fall more heavily upon women in business than upon men. Many wealthy men have failed, even filing bankruptcy several times, along the way to success. Since men are socialized to have more confidence than women, it seems to be easier for them to pick themselves up, brush themselves off, and try again. On the other hand, obstacles for women in the financial world are usually greater; they are frequently very careful to manage their assets in a conservative fashion that makes it unlikely that they will ever have to undergo that difficult climb again.

Women, Wealth, and Power

There are a number of interesting and somewhat disheartening aspects of the relationship between women, wealth, and power. As discussed, it is generally assumed that women have less power than men, both in the business world and in personal relationships. Top positions in business, industry, and government represent great potential power, and people in these positions have many opportunities to exercise that authority. Although industry has slowly and reluctantly begun to take its first steps toward a more equal distribution of power, these highly sought after positions are still primarily the province of men, usually from upper-class, wealthy families. In fact, wealth frequently precedes these positions rather than being the result of them.[13]

Women born into wealth are disproportionately underrepresented among the extremely affluent and powerful. One of the reasons for this is that women who do have access to great wealth are often unable to translate these resources into positions of power and prominence to the same degree as men, because of the many obstacles they face in the male-dominated business world. A. Tickamyer concludes that control of wealth, rather than ownership alone, is the key factor in access to power. Money alone is clearly not sufficient.[14]

In the sixties, a popular theory arose that wealthy women, because they outlived their husbands, controlled the economy. This belief turned out to be true only in a sort of perverted sense. At that time, these women were actually functioning primarily as "conduits for passing power to children, especially sons and sons-in-law."[15] The real power and decision-making lay in the hands of first their husbands then (invariably male) trustees, who were sometimes helpful but often condescending and abrupt, telling the women as little as possible about their money to ensure that they retained the power. Steinem quotes one woman, (possibly a relative of mine!), who said, "If General Motors is going to pass through your womb, they make damn sure you can't grab it on the way through!"[16] In my own life, I find it telling that all four of my financial advisors—my tax attorney, my stockbroker, my accountant, and my financial consultant—are men. Although the final decisions are mine to make, I inevitably rely a great deal upon their advice. In essence, they "control" my wealth. In my case, this happened by chance and probably because the odds are in favor of it; I have always chosen my financial advisors by ability, not gender.

Women are often discounted in terms of their accomplishments and abilities. Therefore, for wealthy, ambitious women, it is even more confusing to know for which "sin" they are being punished. Because of this, the affluent women whom I have interviewed, when choosing a career, almost always pick one in which their wealth is irrelevant—a career that "money can't buy." Julilly Kohler's comment was typical:

> I think one of the reasons that I chose the law, unconsciously, was that you can't be judged that way. In law you're judged on whether you do a good job for your client. But up until that point, basically, I think they discounted women in general. So it's

very hard to figure out which is which. The first time I ever went to visit a man's college for a weekend in my sophomore year, I felt that I had come to a different planet.... There was a difference in the relationship between the teachers and the students at a men's college and the teachers and students at a women's college. It was like we were kindergartners. There was no interaction; there was no real discussion. It was there that I had my first glimmer of what the women's issues were like. That was in 1962. I started realizing that all my issues weren't personal. The first time I decided to become a lawyer was in the sixth grade. I think that anything else I've done, other than law, that it doesn't count ... because people say, "Oh, she can do that because she doesn't have to work or clean a house."

In the continuing struggle for true equality, all women must work a little harder to prove that they can do the same job as well as men. That's not news to us. What may be a disconcerting new awareness is the knowledge that if you are a woman with money and power, your accomplishments will be even more adamantly discounted and denied. With deep sadness, I admit that this resentment comes as frequently from women as it does from men. Although a function of male-female stereotypes, this censure is also a result of the individual's relative sense of security in her own financial, professional, or even personal positions.

Men, Women, and Status

Although most men claim they do not defer to whichever person has the higher status in any given situation, in the end they usually do. One study shows that men are much more unconsciously tuned in to hierarchical behavior and rules than women are.[17] For example, when approached by a well-dressed decoy asking for money to make a phone call, men were more likely to acquiesce than when they were approached by the same person dressed less affluently. Since people are able to conveniently overlook their own conformist tendencies, most men seem to be able to go through life entertaining the myth that the status system is imposed upon them, existing in spite of their many and continuous attempts to frustrate it.

On the other hand, the women in this study were more honest about their behaviors toward people of higher status, acknowledging that such a thing existed and that they were partially responsible for the system that created such inequalities.[18] So, although half of our population acknowledges their contributions in creating the class system, the other half firmly denies their investment in its continuation. Denial is a sure way to ensure the perpetuation of a highly unjust social class system.

Denial and gender bias are still prevalent in our beliefs and behaviors around money, gender, and power. This chapter has shown how common gender differences are accentuated and heightened by the presence of wealth. I hope that a greater awareness of these inequalities and an acknowledgment of the unfairness of the system will enable us all to begin to consciously alter our treatment of one another in the financial war between the genders. When we can begin to support one another based not upon gender and competition, but upon the depth of knowledge each of us has to contribute, the business world will become an entirely different place—one aimed at and based upon a "win-win" strategy.

NOTES

1. John Sedgwick, *Rich Kids* (New York: William Morrow and Company, 1985), 158.

2. Gloria Steinem, "The Trouble with Rich Women," *Ms.*, June 1986, 78.

3. Ibid., 78.

4. Ibid., 78.

5. Anonymous woman, quoted in Steinem, "The Trouble with Rich Women," 78.

6. Ibid, 42.

7. Steinem, "The Trouble with Rich Women," 43.

8. Ibid., 78.

9. Ibid., 42.

10. Sedgwick, *Rich Kids,* 162.

11. Ibid., 163.

12. P. L Menchik, "Is the Family Wealth Squandered? A Test of the Merry-widow Model," *Journal of Economic History* 44, no. 3 (1984): 835–38.

13. A. R. Tickamyer, "Wealth and Power: A Social Comparison of Men and Women in the Property Elite," *Social Forces* 60, no. 2 (1981): 463–81.

14. Ibid., 478–79.

15. Steinem, "The Trouble with Rich Women," 43.

16. Ibid., 43.

17. Henry C. Lindgren, *Great Expectations: The Psychology of Money* (Los Altos, Calif.: William Kaufman, 1980), 73.

18. Ibid., 70–72, 96–97.

6

"NOT INHALING":
THE PYRAMID
OF SHAME

Toxic shame . . . is an excruciatingly internal experience of unexpected exposure. It is a deep cut felt primarily from the inside. It divides us from ourselves and from others. In toxic shame, we disown ourselves. And this disowning demands a cover-up. Toxic shame parades in many garbs and get-ups. It loves darkness and secretiveness.

JOHN BRADSHAW
Healing the Shame That Binds You

FOR THOSE OF US STRUGGLING WITH AFFLUENZA and other afflictions of the self and soul, our core fear is that if we look inside ourselves, what we see there will not be good enough. This message of shame that many of us carry is that there is somehow something *wrong* with us; we are somehow *wrong;* intrinsically and irreparably. Emotional damage done during our childhood development leaves us believing that we were created flawed and that there is nothing we can do to fix ourselves. Nurturing this misconception is the suspicion that everyone else was created better than we were. Together, these ideas and false beliefs feed our shame; at the same time they compel us to cover it up at all costs. Thus, hidden from conscious consideration, the main function of shame becomes to *drive* us—away from knowledge of our true selves. Shame pushes us toward anything that will, for the moment, obscure the unpleasant realities of our lives: our imperfections, our weaknesses, and ultimately, our mortality. When we live with this kind of feeling, we avoid more than just the bleakness of our own existence; we drop our eyes to avoid the horror of poverty and homelessness that are part of our *cultural* shame. Unable to face the monkey on our own back, we become totally paralyzed and incapable of confronting or changing our society's soul sickness. When we look into the eyes of another, all we can see reflected is our own anguish.

Because we believe that we are flawed beyond redemption, it becomes a matter of survival for us to create a false Self. Alice Miller calls this process "soul murder." The farther we turn away from our authentic selves, the more we cease to exist psychologically. The creation of a false identity dovetails neatly with today's cultural emphasis on external appearances, and we become shame-bound. Bradshaw writes, "The shame binding of feelings, needs and natural instinctual drives is a key factor in changing healthy shame into toxic shame. To be shame-bound means that whenever you feel any feeling, any need or any drive, you immediately feel ashamed."[1]

When shame becomes enmeshed with the dysfunctional patterns of accumulating and possessing wealth, the affluent become increasingly shame-bound. From the Family Founder who is subtly enabled by his family to work endless hours in pursuit of greater and greater wealth, to the shy rich child who is forced to perform and achieve to be considered successful, to the obese debutante whose self-image and aspirations are based on dictums like, "You can never be too rich, or too thin," the culture of wealth, perhaps more than any other culture in our society, encourages us to be anything other than ourselves. With the never-ending push for perfection common among affluents, we have become a class of "soul murderers" and the "soul murdered."

Perfectionism results when we value ourselves or others for achievement only: a human "doing," rather than a human "being." Again, the extreme emphasis on externals that is a part of the affluent world is a perfect setup for the formation of an entire class of perfectionists. It is a logical extension of our false selves. Since we are creating what we think we *should* be in these other selves, there are no boundaries to our expectations of ourselves or others. "Good enough" becomes "perfect," and we *must* be perfect in order to be acceptable. For the Family Founder who suffers from perfectionism, there is never "enough" money.

In chapter 3, we discussed the narcissistic personality disorder and how it is frequently discovered in the Family Founder or within the family structure of the affluent. Under the heading, *Character Disorder Syndromes of Shame,* Bradshaw writes, "The Narcissist is endlessly motivated to seek perfection in everything he does. Such a personality is driven to the acquisition of wealth, power and beauty, and to find others who will mirror and admire his grandiosity. Underneath this external facade there is an emptiness filled with envy and rage. The core of this emptiness is internalized shame."[2]

Bradshaw identifies another face of toxic shame frequently

found among the affluent: grandiosity. Grandiosity is a disorder of the will, a part of the false self. It manifests as "much greater than" or "much smaller than" thinking: each judgment of others made in relation to ourselves, a distortion of reality. The will is disabled by the shaming of the emotions. Bradshaw describes some of the problems caused by this state of disablement, which sound similar to the presenting symptoms of many of my affluenza clients.

> The will wills what can't be willed.
> The will tries to control everything.
> The will experiences itself as omnipotent or when it has failed as "wormlike."
> The will wills for the sake of willing (impulsiveness).
> The will wills in absolute extremes—all or nothing.[3]

It is easy to see where toxic shame might begin to form in the affluent household. According to Erik Erikson, it is in the second stage of psychosocial development that we begin to develop a sense of shame.[4] In the first stage, a child develops a basic sense of trust. Following naturally, in a healthy household, is the formation of an interpersonal bond, which forms a bridge of mutuality between a child and his or her primary caretaker. As previously discussed, the only way children have of developing a sense of self and the ability to recognize their feelings is through accurate and caring mirroring by their caretakers. Wealthy children raised by surrogate caretakers are at high risk for the interpersonal bond to be incorrectly formed (or not formed at all), depending on the reliability and trustworthiness of the surrogate parent. The bottom line is that the surrogate is *not* the parent and does not have the depth of caring or emotional investment in the child that a healthy, involved parent does.

If the caretaker is adequate to create the basic bond of trust, according to Erikson, the child is now in a position to develop healthy or toxic shame, again depending on the psychological health of the primary caretaker. The psychosocial task for this stage is to strike a balance between autonomy, shame, and doubt.[5] The most crucial need during this phase is for the caretaker to set good boundaries and limits. If a child is loved unconditionally at this stage, i.e., if he or she is allowed to explore and test limits without the destruction of the interpersonal bridge, then the child develops healthy shame. It is also of the utmost importance for the caretaker to model and mirror healthy shame, boundaries, and limits. Herein lies the second opportunity for toxic shame to develop.

If the wealthy child is being raised primarily by surrogate caretakers, it is highly unlikely that they will continue to love the child unconditionally in the face of the repeated temper tantrums that only a two-year-old knows how to throw. This is a time when many loving parents are tested beyond their endurance level. It is asking a lot to expect even parents to respond lovingly and appropriately at all times. When we demand that hired people love our children as we do, we are expecting the near impossible from them, because the parent-child bond is absent from their relationship. One of two things is likely to happen at this juncture. The surrogate caretaker will either harshly reprimand and shame the child for any display of "unseemly" behavior because it is not acceptable in affluent society, or the caretaker will simply refuse to put up with such behavior and take action to make very sure it isn't repeated. Any unpleasant display of a "negative" feeling is summarily and repeatedly punished and shamed, causing these feelings to become shame-bound in the future.

Another possibility is a more subtle form of shaming that takes place frequently when children are raised by someone other than their parents: the lack of *any* kind of response from the caretaker. In this instance, the child develops neither healthy shame nor toxic shame until a later developmental stage, when many of his or her emotional patterns of response may already be dangerously dysfunctional, threatening healthy survival. Of course, lack of care-taking cuts across all socioeconomic lines and has even more dev-astating results when combined with the unmet survival needs of the poor and homeless. For the wealthy child, however, this con-tributes to the silver-spoon syndrome discussed earlier. No healthy limits are set for these children and, therefore, they learn none. Their own two-year-old behaviors become the role models for their future personality development.

In a dysfunctional wealthy home, there is a good chance that the parents are shame-based; toxic shame is at the core of most dysfunctional behavior. In the event that shame-bound parents are present in the household and actually take an active role in child rearing, the child will begin to identify with their shame-based models, another powerful and damaging way for toxic shame to become internalized. According to Bradshaw, shame in-ternalization involves at least three processes, all of which are highly likely to be present in a family suffering from affluenza:

1. Identification with unreliable and shame-based models.
2. The trauma of abandonment, and the binding of feel-ings, needs, and drives with shame.
3. The interconnection of memory imprints, which form collages of shame.[6]

The last process refers simply to repeated shamings, which in the adult are brought whole to one's emotional consciousness by the trigger of a single incident that reminds one of the initial shaming.

Toxic shame hides easily in the guise of wealth. It is often the foundation of the Family Founder's workaholism or desire to be noticed. Certainly it weaves itself throughout the question of spending, buying, and philanthropy; it is attached to the money, both incoming and outgoing. Perhaps it has come wrapped up in the very means by which the money is earned. Is one's fortune "dirty" money, tainted with the sweat and blood of people who were sacrificed in the act of accumulating it?

For those of us who inherit wealth, there is shame in the knowledge that we did not earn it and yet can spend it for our own pleasure. Shame and confusion underlie the question, "Why me?" The nature of this question, regardless of what it might refer to in our personal experience, implies separation from others. Whether our wealth separates us from others for "good reasons" such as being able to afford an expensive and extensive education, or "bad reasons" such as buying expensive, potentially fatal drugs in large quantities, it nevertheless sets us apart. Toxic shame, by its very definition, has already severed us from ourselves. Bradshaw writes:

> Toxic shame, the shame that binds you, is experienced as the all-pervasive sense that I am flawed and defective as a human being. Toxic shame is no longer an emotion that signals our limits, it is a state of being, a core identity. Toxic shame gives you a sense of worthlessness, a sense of failing and falling short as a human being. Toxic shame is a rupture of the self with the self.[7]

So, where does this leave us? We have been separated from ourselves and others by a supposed gift that we are not sure we deserve, and from a parent or relative with whom we may or may not have had a healthy relationship. In addition, this gift causes others to regard us with envy, anger, and sometimes outright hatred. And yet outright hatred is a lot easier to deal with than obsequious, pandering, overly polite behavior that disguises the deeper feelings of loathing. Is it any wonder that the wealthy are left holding an "empty bag," as Ted Turner put it? I would suggest that the bag in fact is *not* empty, but filled with toxic shame.

Going deeper, the shame grows for the affluent as a by-product of knowing that they are really *not* better than the nonaffluent. In fact, their personal shame-based message would have them believe that they, the affluent, lack the strength of character forged in the struggle for survival and are, therefore, "worse" than the person of average means. In order to deliver themselves from the cognitive dissonance this engenders, wealthy people struggle to find ways to make themselves equal. There are many strategies the rich employ to bring themselves into alignment with this disparity. They may overcompensate for their wealth by surrendering other parts of themselves. They may give when they don't want to give. They may do what others want them to do rather than being true to themselves, lest others think them "rich snobs." They may pretend to be nice to people they might not particularly like for the same reason.

For those of us who are wealthy, this situation is a psychological catch-22. We silently implore you to like us, *in spite of the fact that we are rich*. We behave as though this substance, money, that makes us so different is a deformity or handicap, which in truth it sometimes is. And yet, because of the perpetuation of the myth surrounding money and happiness, we are fooled into carrying this lie, this pretense of fulfillment, as though it were the truth. More toxic shame is created and reinforced in the very travesty of this lie, for toxic shame can only prosper in the darkness of the unexamined mind and the unexpressed heart. When we bring it into the light, look at it, and tell the truth about it, eventually it can no longer hold us in its power.

However, it is extremely difficult to challenge such deep-seated cultural messages. Rather than say to ourselves, "Maybe money really doesn't guarantee happiness," and follow that belief through to its logical conclusion—which would probably entail massive behavioral and lifestyle changes—we turn it in upon ourselves and say, "What's wrong with me that this wonderful, sought-after substance, money, isn't making me happy?" We look everywhere else for the reason behind our misery.

Even if we begin to suspect that perhaps our unhappiness is tied somehow to our wealth, we must step cautiously. For it is *not* the money itself that fails to deliver the promised paradise; it is the *way* we use the money, the intent behind it, the level of consciousness with which we operate our financial affairs that does or does not bring us peace of mind and affirm our souls. It is hard at best, and impossible at worst, to bring our personal truth about wealth in alignment when the entire society is in a state of cognitive dissonance and denial about affluence.

For the ambitious individuals who work long and hard for their wealth, the disillusionment they feel when and if they finally discover that their money has not purchased happiness and self-esteem can be doubly hard to bear. They know how much time, effort, and personal sacrifice has gone into securing their "success." On talk shows, at Twelve Step meetings, and in my office, I hear a great many middle-aged men and women who have become disappointed and depressed, often turning to alcohol, drugs, or food in a vain attempt to alleviate their disenchantment with the American dream. Left with most of the same problems they had before they became wealthy, and a few additional ones that came with the new territory, they begin to realize with horror and shame that they have sold their souls for the sake of a buck. Along with their souls they have frequently left their families behind in the dust of their obsessive climb to wealth. They are left alone with their guilt and shame—or more accurately, they join the rest of society in carrying our cultural toxic shame about money and wealth.

Shame vs. Guilt

Shame is a core feeling. It is about who we feel we are in our deepest being. Guilt is very closely aligned with shame, but is rightfully about something we've *done*. The two emotions are frequently confused. When we talk about feeling guilty, we are often speaking of shame. Guilt feelings can sometimes be assuaged by making amends to the injured party. Feelings of shame are seldom that easily erased.

When I asked the people I interviewed to talk about their net worth, one of the most frequently mentioned feelings was guilt. It is my belief that what they were describing would more accurately be defined as toxic shame. In *Rich Kids*, Sedgwick writes, "Rich kids soon recognize the miserable truth: for them to be so extraordinarily rich, others must be poor."[8] Because inheritance is entirely passive, it bypasses guilt and becomes shame. Criminals who are guilty of a crime, "doing" something wrong, can reform and receive forgiveness. The inheritor hasn't "done" anything, and therefore there is no absolution. Their only crime is one of being, and so their guilt becomes about them and who they are. They begin to feel as if they personify their guilt — in essence, the definition of toxic shame — and that "every crime that was ever committed out of greed now hangs on their heads. Because they are on top, they must be squashing those on the bottom."[9] As penance, they may cultivate misery or, ashamed of their largesse and how they got it, they may make hefty donations to charity. In an attempt to sublimate their shame, they may decide to exclude people of average income from their lives and choose to associate solely with their "own class." In this way, they somehow hope to avoid being reminded of their shame and the people on the bottom. This tribalism is also an effective way to avoid the "wealthism," or covert prejudice, they sense from those who are not wealthy. This exclusion of "others" also allows the wealthy to hoard more, develop a false sense of moral superiority, and generally remove themselves from much of the unpleasantness of everyday life: all actions or feelings that increase their shame.

Setting Healthy Boundaries

Toxic shame, rather than — or in addition to — genuine caring, may drive the hand that signs the donation checks. It may also stimulate another common emotion associated with charitable giving—anger. This anger stems from the fact that the public's perception of one's wealth often far outweighs the reality. The hand is always out, the phone always rings at dinner time, and the requests for money take up the majority of room in the mailbox. Having given an amount with which one is rarely comfortable (Is it too little or too much?), affluent individuals discover that their donations are expected to increase over time. Instead of being left alone for a period following their generous act, they find the requests increasing in frequency and the expectation of a greater donation next time. Though solicitations are not made only of the wealthy, it is hardly surprising that the frequency and number of requests to the rich is far greater than those made to the nonaffluent.

Learning to say "no," or asking for time to think about it, is an important step in letting go of the guilt and shame. It also plays a part in the larger issue of learning to set personal boundaries around what is healthy and what we are willing and not willing to do. It allows us time for reflection and self-examination. Through a thoughtful, feeling-based process, we can decide if our inclination to give or not to give is coming from our hearts or from our legacy of shame. If it is from the latter, our saying, "no" becomes an important part not only in letting go of our shame, but also in refusing to take it on in the first place. We are no longer willing to make decisions from a fear-based, shame-driven, and unconscious position. When we give from our hearts, the feeling of joy is clear. When we give because we feel as if we have to, or we *should*, our emotional state becomes clouded, angry, and tinged with resentment and shame.

The Shame of "Shoulds"

"Shoulds" are irrevocably tied with shame. They are generally childhood messages and were born on the point of Mom or Dad's finger, shaken in our faces with the message, implicit or explicit, that we were "bad" little boys or girls. There are countless "shoulds" trussed tightly to nearly every money message we receive from our parents, other benefactors, and society. It becomes a lengthy and confusing task to unravel the shame from these messages, but only by being willing to do so can we discover what is true for us and what is not. If and when we are clear of the toxic shame, when our feelings are no longer shame-bound, we can begin to make decisions about our behavior and the behavior of others based on how we really think and feel.

The discord between how we think we should feel and how we do feel frequently causes us to feel guilt, or worse, shame. After all, we should really feel the way we think, right? Our hearts and souls, however, have a strong will of their own, and feelings can rarely be thought away. For example, the "Big boys don't cry" message that many men received as children has wrought immeasurable harm on generations of men who now struggle to experience and assimilate their sorrow and grief. When men feel the shame of the present, the toxic shame of their childhood feelings are also triggered, making their present experience doubly hard to bear and reinforcing their unconscious, or conscious, decision not to cry. Unexpressed grief wreaks havoc in their lives in the form of depression, addictions, rage, and innumerable other dysfunctions of the inauthentic self. Frequently, it manifests in an inability to form or sustain lasting, intimate relationships. This is only one of the byproducts of toxic shame; nevertheless, it relegates a large portion of our population to lives of loneliness and despair.

Because of the strong cultural and familial messages about money, it is doubtful that we will initially attribute our unhappiness or discontent to our beliefs about wealth or our use of money. Uncomfortable with the guilt or shame associated with our feelings, and probably unaware of its source, we begin looking for a cause, for someone or something to blame. If we are in an intimate relationship, we often blame our partner; if not our love partner, then our business partner, or *someone*. One frequent hazard in all relationships is the displacement of feelings such as anger, resentment, grief, and fear—all feelings frequently shamed by childhood caretakers as disruptive, uncivilized, or unbecoming of our class. A feeling becomes displaced when it is repressed or not expressed at the appropriate time, and then is later "placed" inappropriately and disproportionately, often on the wrong person.

Shame from Past Relationships

Sometimes we express anger toward our partner when it is not our partner with whom we are angry, but a significant other from our past who has somehow let us down. How can we know for sure that this is happening? If our emotional reaction to a current situation is out of proportion to what the situation calls for, we can almost always assume that we are tapping into unresolved issues from past relationships. Just knowing that this possibility exists can often help us to find a healthier way to release our feelings. If, as women, we are embarrassed that our partner doesn't work in a higher-power, higher-paying profession, we might, upon closer examination, realize that it's not our partner whom we are ashamed of, but our own father who didn't support us, either emotionally or financially; our anger has become repressed and shame-bound. Perhaps we are embarrassed about *ourselves* because our culture tells us that if we were worthy enough, smart enough, and beautiful enough, we would be able to attract a more "successful" man. Both of these messages are shame-based. One we inappropriately inflict upon our partner. The other is inflicted on us by our own culture to the extent that we choose to accept such an assessment. If we want to understand why we are having problems in our intimate relationships, it helps to look carefully at our covert beliefs about success—how and where our definition of a happy, fulfilling, successful life was born. What follows is one client's successful attempt to confront the shame, anger, and disenchantment she felt following her husband's inheritance.

Sara's Story

As we have seen, it is often difficult for a man to have a positive relationship with a woman who is financially more well off than he is. It is sometimes equally difficult for a woman from a middle-class background to adjust to sudden success or wealth and all of the cultural demands and expectations that come with it.

I had a client named Sara who had been raised in a hard-working, self-made family. There had never been a lot of money, but the small family business enabled them to live comfortably. Sara married Peter, who came from a fairly wealthy background but was not living an affluent lifestyle when they met because he had not inherited any of the money yet. Several years after they were married and had two children, Peter's aunt died and left them a substantial sum. Sara's situation was further compounded by her knowledge that, when Peter's mother died, they would inherit yet another fortune.

Sara had no idea how this supposedly positive windfall would affect her happy marriage. Like most of us, she assumed the money would enhance her family's life and was reluctant to believe otherwise, even when things began to fall apart. In cases such as this, I have observed that people often go through a period of denial before they realize that it is the unconscious negative effects of wealth that wreak such havoc in their lives. For example, Sara had been comfortable in their middle-class neighborhood, surrounded by friends who shared her values, work ethic, and hobbies. She felt out of place in her new affluent neighborhood, and her friends from the old neighborhood were ill at ease in her new, designer-decorated home. Peter was struggling with his own wealth-related issues at work, and was not emotionally available to Sara, which compounded her feelings of loneliness and isolation.

Things were difficult for Peter as well. When Sara and Peter moved into a larger house in an affluent neighborhood, his previously fulfilling job as a social worker in a mental health facility began to pale in comparison to the movers and shakers who inhabited the surrounding mansions. Although their lifestyle bespoke affluence, the type of job Peter had and the fact that Sara didn't work made it obvious that their money was inherited — that Peter hadn't made the fortune on his own. As Peter compared himself to those around him, his feelings of inadequacy grew as his self-esteem and self-worth declined, and he soon fell into a deep depression. No longer comfortable with his co-workers, somehow ashamed of his inheritance, he kept it a secret, knowing that their attitudes toward him would shift drastically when they found out about the money and the big house in the suburbs.

Sara pushed her own growing feelings of discomfort aside to help Peter through his painful time of depression. There were also a lot of questions from the children that she felt ill-equipped and hesitant to answer, questions such as, "Are we rich?" and, "How much money do we have?" When Peter got back on his feet again, Sara suddenly discovered that she was angry and resentful that her feelings had been repressed and, she felt, not taken into account. After all, she was the one who was left at home with the children and thrown into uncomfortable discussions with the neighborhood wives and mothers, with whom she felt she had little in common. Peter had begun to confide in a few of his friends and was beginning to feel less isolated and depressed. As he felt better, however, Sara felt worse. It was during this period that she came to see me for counseling for her newfound affluenza.

Sara is an attractive, well-adjusted young woman; but the cognitive dissonance she was experiencing in her life left her feeling confused, angry, uncomfortable, and ashamed. Society and our cultural beliefs dictated that Sara should be happy with her good fortune—literally a fortune! The feelings she was experiencing, however, were anything but happy. Her covert and overt belief systems were also in direct conflict with her new life. Her family heritage was based upon a traditional Midwest work ethic that said people had to earn what they received in life. She felt shame and unworthiness in the face of this unearned wealth. What made things worse was that the church she and Peter belonged to had long ridiculed the wealthy, considering it more "holy" to live in poverty. The myth that one must be poor to be truly spiritual is a debilitating and limiting belief to which many religions still adhere; "blessed are the poor. . . ." Fearing her church's disapproval, Sara had kept the "good" news of their inheritance a shameful secret from a group that, until that time, she had considered her closest support. Since she didn't fit into the neighborhood clique of affluent wives, she became lonely and isolated. In addition, her job as a teacher, which had given her identity and self-esteem, had been cut from the school budget the previous year. She was no longer needed, not a pleasant feeling for anyone.

Sara and I began her therapy sessions with a discussion of affluenza: what it is, how it works in the family system, what the symptoms are, what to tell the children about the money, and so on. Sara was an eager and bright learner and felt immediate relief to discover that she was neither crazy nor alone in her suffering. I gave her the unfinished manuscript of this book to read, and she came back the following week feeling more optimistic about her future. Next we spent some time unearthing her covert beliefs, searching out those that were shame-based and bringing them out into the open where we could honestly assess their validity. Throughout our sessions, Sara had immediate access to her feelings and was able to cry frequently about her loneliness and isolation. It was more difficult, however, for us to reach the anger and shame that we both knew were there.

The turning point for Sara came one day during an experiential therapeutic exercise aimed at helping her get to her hidden anger and resentment—the foundation of her shame. This therapy was a combination of the "empty chair" exercise and role reversal. In the empty chair exercise the client sits opposite an empty chair and talks to whomever or whatever he or she wants or needs to address. In this case I taped currency all over the back of the chair, enabling Sara to actually talk to her husband's inheritance. She began to cry almost immediately, expressing her frustration and disbelief at the "betrayal" she felt. Her tears soon turned into anger and she screamed and cried, stomping her feet and pounding the arms of the chair with her clenched fists. She was furious that the money had "let her down," failing to "make her happy" as she had hoped and believed it would. Gathering steam, she screamed her rage at the negative effects of her supposed good fortune. Not only were her own beliefs about wealth totally inaccurate, but she also had to combat her old friends' and family's opinions on how she *should* handle the money, how it *should* make her feel—and their disappointment when she didn't feel or act the way they thought she should. She cried, screamed, and raged until her anger was gone, and the emotional charge surrounding her inheritance began to dissipate.

After her emotional release, I asked her to reverse roles with her wealth, which meant changing chairs and "becoming" the money. I then instructed Sara, as the money, to tell Sara, as the empty chair, why wealth was in her life and what purpose it served. When Sara had this conversation with wealth, she was able to see the inheritance for what it was—a substance that could be transformed into whatever she wished. Slowly, the money lost its control of her and she began to learn to control it. She was no longer simply reacting to wealth in seemingly random emotional ways, but was taking a proactive stand in her relationship to it. Her recovery was rapid from that point on and, before long, our mutually beneficial sessions came to an end. As always, I learned and grew as much as Sara did in the few short months we worked together.

Money, Power, and Shame

For most of us, affluent or not, money holds a dimension of power. The more money an individual has, the more power she or he is perceived as having. People generally resent and distrust those who have more power than they do. This gap of mistrust between the rich and the poor is made even more visible by the media. As one author wrote, "Those who are neither rich nor poor—the rest of 'us'—cannot read the daily newspaper without a sense of outrage. Both the lazy irresponsible rich and the lazy irresponsible poor seem constantly to be taking advantage of 'us.'"[10]

Because the rich are generally aware of how others feel about them, they sometimes maintain a very low profile. Millionaire ranchers may wear worn work clothes and drive old, battered pickup trucks because those behaviors are consistent with their values of frugality and maintaining a healthy humility. If, however, they are more the result of unconscious attempts to "blend in" with the nonaffluent, these same behaviors may indicate deeper feelings of unworthiness. Strategies to hide wealth are often unconscious efforts to keep feelings of shame at bay. Even if they have "made it" on their own, but particularly if their money is "unearned" income, they may have feelings of shame connected with having so much when others have so little. Often feeling helpless and powerless—after all, how much can one person do to ease the suffering of the poor?—they shamefully retreat into anonymity, avoiding the spotlight of appearing rich.

Prejudice against the rich is seen again in the difference between the "quality" of gift giving between the rich and the poor.

When a poor person gives gifts to another poor person, our culture perceives them as generously sharing scanty resources with one another. When a rich person gives a poor person a gift, it is often regarded with suspicion, as if the giver were using the gift as a means to impress the recipient with his or her power.[11] When the poor person shares, the person who receives the gift feels comforted and reassured. Ironically, the same gift from a wealthy person can create discomfort, ingratitude, and distrust in the receiver. The receiver may well feel patronized. Granted, gifts from wealthy people who are addicted to power and manipulation may have humiliating and demeaning strings attached. Nevertheless, from the perspective of the affluent, they are damned if they do and damned if they don't.

Sometimes the feelings of power and control that come with having money are so strong that they overwhelm those who earn it or inherit it. When one has a great deal of money, one's life is often devoid of structure or boundaries. An endless continuum of choices breeds depression; the wealthy may perceive their lives as out of control. They begin to feel as if the money is something that is happening *to* them and that their wishes have little, if any, effect upon the outcome. This lack of control also reinforces toxic shame. Relief comes from the realization that they do have some control over the choices. Even the smallest step in a positive direction can be the beginning of finding a healthy balance.

As the next story illustrates, the confusion and shame contained in the creation of wealth can lead even the most educated and well-meaning of people into financial disaster—which could, of course, be a blessing in disguise.

Not Inhaling

Lee Jampolsky, author of *Healing the Addictive Mind, The Art of Trust* and *Listen to Me . . .* , recently shared how his wounded early relationship with his then emotionally unavailable, alcoholic father affected how he later handled his own financial success. When his father, Gerald Jampolsky, author of *Love Is Letting Go of Fear*, went into recovery and became successful, Lee's anger and resentment toward him grew. Although Lee was also a recovering addict, that all-important father-son relationship remained unhealed at that time, and Lee became convinced that his father's newfound spiritual path, reflected in his writings and workshops, was a sham. The fact that people held his father in such high esteem and so valued his work poured salt onto an already festering wound. It was years before Lee could see the genuineness of his father's changes. Prior to that time, however, Lee's anger and frustration led him to measure his own success primarily in terms of financial possessions.

However, while doubting the validity of his father's work, Lee came to sense that his own financial achievements might be hollow as well. Seeing himself reflected in his father, Lee's monetary success unconsciously became tainted with feelings of shame.

Thus began his complex and dysfunctional relationship with wealth, or as Lee calls it, his personal version of "not inhaling." He wanted to use his financial resources without acknowledging them; he wanted the "high" without admitting that he was using the "drug," without dirtying his consciousness by having a relationship with the money. In spite of his growing uneasiness with wealth, in a type of blind denial, Lee allowed himself to make lots of money. By this point he had earned his Ph.D. in psychology, had a rapidly growing private practice, and was a successful author in his own right. He had no problem spending what he earned. He owned two homes, a private plane, and many other material possessions that spoke of his economic station in life.

However, his relationship with the money he earned stopped at spending it. Unacknowledged and unexamined toxic shame prevented Lee from directly handling the substance. He turned over the entire management of the family finances to his wife. Several years later, when the marriage began to unravel, he discovered that due to his denial and poor financial communication with his wife, the financial security that he had taken for granted was nonexistent. Most of the money was gone and he was forced to start over financially. All the "toys" had to be sold and Lee faced the painful truth about his particular case of affluenza. Realizing that he has been given a second chance to create a healthy relationship with money, he is carefully, consciously, and cautiously deciding what his financial future will look like.

The Shame of the "Idle Rich"

Lack of the traditional career structure, particularly the absence of the necessity to work, combined with grandiose guidelines and expectations in many rich people's lives, make it important for a wealthy person to take extra care in creating a unique, workable lifestyle. One of the most difficult parts in this process is recognizing and altering the message of shame that is implicit in not working—or, more specifically, in not having a job. Given the life expectancy of the average person today, and the financial uncertainty of these times, it is not unusual for any man or woman to go through periods of joblessness for whatever reason. However, some reasons for not working are culturally acceptable and some are frowned upon or discredited. High on that latter list is the young person who inherits a fortune and chooses to either quit his or her job or not get one. Consequently, wealthy people often feel compelled to prove to the world that they are, in fact, "working"; e.g., the society matron's hectic philanthropic activities, a wealthy heir creating and going to an "office" or studio that is totally useless and unnecessary.

The cultural assumption is that one finds purpose and meaning in life through his or her occupation or job; that in order to make a contribution to society one must work. The problem is, there is little latitude given to the definition of "work" in our culture. How is toxic shame generated in affluents by these assumptions? I'll give you an example within my own family.

I have a cousin who inherited a comfortable sum from an aunt of ours who died several years ago. Struggling with a variety of addictions, failed relationships, and finally his own failed business, he chose to go into a Twelve Step program for treatment and began his recovery journey. During this time, he either didn't hold a job or held entry-level, minimum wage positions. Contrary to what most of our family and friends thought, he worked very hard during the several years that he didn't hold a well-paying job. Spiritually, emotionally, and physically, he is a different person today. His ability to "contribute" to society, whether he ever held another job or not, has multiplied a hundred-fold. He is a better father, a better friend, and a happier, more contented human being.

Recently, I asked him how it felt when he wasn't working. He said he felt ashamed because he knew what others thought of him. It was difficult at times, not just to keep his faith in God and a greater plan, but to keep his faith in *himself* in the face of the opinions of others. Family comments such as, "I'm the only one in this family supporting his wife and kids," and, "Well, someone has to work," steadily eroded his confidence and self-worth and added greatly to his struggle to continue on his chosen path. I am happy to say that he recently took a position back at the top of his original profession, better able now in every way to support himself, his family, and society as a whole.

A personal friend, Larry, is contemplating quitting his career as an attorney. He has worked for almost twenty years, often night and day, has been divorced twice, has no children to support, and is beginning to wonder what life is all about. He is in recovery for alcoholism and readily admits that he is a workaholic. In addition to his own resistance to giving up his "drug" of choice, he is aware of society's views of people who don't work and is very hesitant to put himself in the hot seat. He sheepishly admits to his own case of wealthism and has started to examine his unfair judgments not only about the wealthy, but about others like himself, who for a period of time, could afford not to have an income.

A final, powerful example of the shame connected to "not working" is seen in the words of countless numbers of therapists who have responded to a wealthy person's search for meaning in life with the answer, "Just find a job." More than one of my clients have breathed a huge sigh of relief when that was not my first response to their quest for self-identity.

These people and these therapists are responding to their own—and society's—unexamined beliefs about work. The truth is that "working" is not about a career or job. We have simply taken the most obvious definition as the right and only one.

Considering that the majority of people work to ensure basic survival, it is not hard to understand why we define "work" by those standards. Nevertheless, if we could just broaden our understanding and definition of worthwhile work, it would lessen the toxic shame that the rich or poor jobless must carry. Work is about making a contribution to society, and there are countless ways of doing that. The spectrum is broad and encompasses all ages and levels of society. From small children who recycle their families' aluminum cans to the powerful CEOs of major corporations, when people use their talents and education to the best of their abilities and for the greater good, then they are "working." Whether one is rich or poor or holds a traditional nine-to-five job does not indicate whether or not they are a contributing, functional part of society.

Not surprisingly, the nonwealthy are frequently jealous of the affluent person's ability to avoid the everyday, often monotonous, job. Because of their jealousy, envy, and resentment, they may criticize and label all wealthy people as the "idle rich." More often than not, however, the nonwealthy would also desire to trade places with the very people they denigrate. To what end do we make such judgments? This lack of honest communication about real feelings incites shame on both sides. The affluent can feel the unspoken animosity and anger and assume they have done something wrong, which creates guilt and shame. They may either internalize it, in which case it may cause physical or emotional misery, or they may externalize it as anger in lashing back at their "tormentors," the nonwealthy. The nonwealthy, on the other hand, wish they could be "idle," and so they continue to direct their resentment toward the wealthy. Both groups frequently hold the erroneous belief that not having to work is preferable and will make the quality of one's life better.

Money as a Tool of Humiliation

There are also tragic consequences for children of poverty in the shaming implications of our cultural holiday traditions, particularly Christmas. "Good" little boys and girls get presents, "bad" ones don't. Therefore, rich kids are by definition "good," while poor kids carry the toxic shame of being labeled "bad." Other holidays are similarly shaming, even though the cultural message may not be as clear. It is always hurtful to a child to stand by empty-handed as his or her wealthy classmates or acquaintances get Easter baskets, Hanukkah gifts, birthday presents, and so on. Many a Family Founder's workaholism and determination to be "successful" (wealthy) is driven by that initial toxic shame.

Of course, shaming cultural assumptions cut both ways across the classes. Humiliation has long been a powerful and cruel weapon of the wealthy who falsely believe they are better than others simply because they have more money. These dysfunctional rich act as though there is a rite of passage, through which only they have passed, which gives them access to information that is desirable and unattainable to the "common" person. It is this potential for humiliation that often makes the nonwealthy wary of the rich. To humiliate someone is to shame them. It is to assume that you know better than they do. The humiliating part for the average person is that it is never quite clear what it is that the rich know better. This situation becomes a no-win scenario for everyone because even if you tried to learn the rules of the game, so to speak, the rules would quickly change and leave you wondering what happened—and feeling even more humiliated because you actually thought for a moment that you understood.

I recently had an eye-opening discussion with a nonwealthy friend named Ted. He shared his fear that if he had dated a rich girl when he was single, he would have somehow been humiliated. "If we were at a dinner party together, I wouldn't have known what fork to use—and she would have laughed at me."

I, on the other hand, spent most of my youth overcompensating for my wealth by allowing men to behave in any way they liked, purposefully *never* risking humiliating them for fear that they wouldn't like me and would think I was a "rich bitch." I have also long carried a deep sense of shame and embarrassment for those wealthy individuals who *do* behave autocratically and snobbishly.

Like many other dysfunctional patterns, the need to humiliate others comes from fear. We are afraid that if we allow others to see us eye to eye, as equals, we will be vulnerable. We are afraid that they won't like what they see. We will then be at risk ourselves to be hurt and humiliated. Our fear comes from being shame-bound and shame-based—a state that originates in the humiliation and hurt of our dysfunctional childhoods. The need to humiliate and shame others and the fear of it happening to us can be transformed when we begin to attach importance to something other than how we look to others on the outside. Critical to this process is the willingness to move away from the belief that what we have or what we do is who we are. When we start to love ourselves and to base our acceptance of ourselves and others on the unconditional love of a higher power, then we begin to experience inner peace, regardless of how we may look to others.

There are many defenses against the felt sense of toxic shame with which an alarming number of the wounded wealthy live. Bradshaw writes about what he labels the "Characterological Styles of Shamelessness": perfectionism, striving for power and control, rage, arrogance, criticism and blame, judgmentalism and moralizing, contempt, patronizing, caretaking and helping, people-pleasing, and envy. It is not that these characteristics *don't* appear in the average population; it is that they seem to appear more often in the wealthy. It is as though money has bestowed on the rich the right to these obnoxious behaviors because they somehow occupy a higher evolutionary ground, as it were. These behaviors of shamelessness not only mark the wealthy individual's feelings of shame, but also transfer them to other people, primarily the nonwealthy. Transferring the shame takes the focus off oneself and places it on someone else, allowing one to avoid the pain associated with toxic shame.

Less annoying to others, but equally as destructive to the suffering individual is another type of shame transference. In this case, the shame is concentrated on a particular part of a person's physical body or external appearance.

I have client named Sue who suffers from affluenza. Periodically, throughout our years of therapy, Sue has fallen back on a unique method that she uses to distract herself when her feelings begin to overwhelm her. She develops a protracted attack of what she and I call "a bad hair day." In spite of the smile that this phrase invokes in most people, this is very serious state of mind for Sue, filling her with great anxiety and driving her relentlessly from hairdresser to hairdresser in search of the perfect haircut. When

Sue is in this state, she is filled with a horrible sense of failure, anger, and anxiety because once again, her efforts to improve her unworthy and unacceptable appearance "didn't work."

Sue's obsession with finding the right appearance has its origin deep in her childhood. Its cause surfaced recently when I was able to help her set some personal boundaries with an old friend to whom she had repeatedly deferred her own better judgment. When Sue was able to see how easy it was for her to knuckle under when her friend criticized the way she looked, dressed, or acted, she was able to understand her haircut obsession for just what it was: a shaming message from her mother that she wasn't pretty enough or good enough on some fundamental level. From this point on, Sue made a commitment to do whatever is necessary in her life to continue to feel good about herself.

A bright, educated, and motivated woman, Sue has known for some time that she disagreed with her affluent world's dictates of what a "successful" lifestyle should or shouldn't be. Every time she tried to break away, however, the old parental messages kept echoing within, despite the fact that both of her parents were dead. These messages shamed her every time she tried to live her life in a manner that made her happier and more satisfied with herself. As Sue began to know herself better and develop more faith in her ability to make wise and healthy decisions, she was able to see the dysfunction in her old behaviors and to put the shame back where it belonged: on her family and "friends" who had used it to control and manipulate her.

The first step in freeing ourselves from shame is to admit our pain to ourselves, to God, and to our family and friends. It is a risk to share our deepest feelings with others. Shame and fear prevent us from turning to one another in honesty and vulnerability. The fear that once again, like our parents, there will be no one there when we ask for help—or worse, that they will respond with anger and derision—keeps the shame alive and thriving. And because we are too afraid to ask, we falsely believe that we are alone in this shame, that we are the only ones who are really this "bad." Whatever we focus our attention on multiplies; what we believe in becomes reality; what we direct our gaze at is all we see. However, it is possible to change our focus.

I believe that if we take the time to look beyond external appearances, really listen to what others say, rich or poor, we will find that we are not so different. A caring act, a generous thought, a simple smile—just the act of meeting another's gaze without dropping one's eyes—all these bring us closer to shedding the shame that we carry as a result of affluenza.

As adults, some of our worst shame is self-inflicted. One of my favorite expressions is, "Put down the stick!" Quit beating yourself up for imagined or real mistakes. Shame *never* does us any good, and guilt seldom does, unless there are legitimate amends to be made to someone.

The first step is always the hardest. But with each little success comes the desire for more. To look for the good and the healthy in another is to find it in ourselves. If we accept others for who they are, regardless of their financial status, rather than shaming them, we will be accepted and valued for who we are.

NOTES

1. John Bradshaw, *Healing the Shame That Binds You* (Deerfield Beach, Fla.: Health Communications, 1988), 12.
2. Ibid., 19.
3. Ibid., 22.
4. Ibid., 19.
5. Ibid., 5.
6. Ibid., 11.

7. Ibid., 10.

8. John Sedgwick, *Rich Kids* (New York: William Morrow and Company, 1985), 106.

9. Ibid., 107.

10. Henry C. Lindgren, *Great Expectations: The Psychology of Money* (Los Alto, Calif.: William Kaufman, 1980), 127.

11. Ibid., 127.

7

MONEY DEAREST:
HEALING FROM AFFLUENZA

Fortune is Janus-faced, first appearing as a captor to be eluded and then as a guide to be befriended. Fortune is first a nemesis, requiring the . . . discontented inheritors to cultivate and execute such active virtues as cunning, bravery, courage, and fortitude. To work out a life of wealth is to work out a moral identity.

NELSON W. ALDRICH JR.
Old Money: The Mythology of America's Upper Class

MANY PEOPLE WHO SUFFER FROM AFFLUENZA hesitate to seek professional help.[1] Since they are wealthy, they believe they don't have the right to complain; they are ashamed of having problems. They cling desperately to the myth that money can and, more importantly, should solve all their difficulties. In reality, they should know better than anyone how painfully untrue that is.

Denial, however, is a powerful foe and money an illusive, deceiving substance. One minute it is your best friend and the next, your worst enemy. As with food, one must learn to use it in moderation. When it is available in large quantities, an "all-you-can-eat" buffet, it is nearly impossible not to overindulge and then suffer the consequences. Whether it be cold cash or credit cards, most of us have the means to indulge ourselves to a lesser or greater degree at one time or another. It alternately satiates us and starves us. Both the super-rich and the would-be rich are awed by the magic web of illusion this powerful substance weaves. Yet individually and culturally, money robs us of our spiritual identity and lulls us into a false sense of security. It is a giant bandage with which we try to cover our wounds, when what we need to be doing is exposing them to the light so they can begin to heal.

As discussed in chapter 6, the wealthy are further immobilized by the shame caused by such comments as, "I wish I had *your* problems!" or, "If your money is such a burden, give it to me. I'll show you how to deal with it," which minimize the psychological complexities involved. Running from this shame, the affluent are desperate to believe, as most people in this country do, that wealth or the pursuit of it couldn't possibly be at the root of their discontent. Again and again, I am amazed at the vehement anger I get in response to my work. Many people, rich or otherwise, are quite offended that I would question the sanctity of the almighty dollar. Others seem to think it either frivolous or downright immoral to expend energy attending to the mental health needs of the wealthy. The subtext of their comment "others are in greater need of help" is really "others are more deserving" or even "the rich are *not* deserving."

On the other hand, there are those whose support and validation make all I do worthwhile. At a recent seminar I gave in Tucson, Arizona, a woman who had remained silent throughout the evening approached me with tears in her eyes after the other participants had left. She said, "Thank God, someone is finally talking about this. My entire family has been destroyed by affluenza."

If you find yourself flying up the corporate ladder, suddenly making more money than you ever dreamed possible, now is the time to change your belief system about what money can and cannot do for you. This chapter can help you find and maintain balance in your life so that you and your family might avoid the many pitfalls of affluenza. Money is only a small part of having a rich life. It is vitally important to leave space in your hectic schedule for the activities that truly enrich the soul. Leave plenty of time to love, laugh, pray, meditate, and to exercise the body, mind, and spirit. Most important, be sure to share your wealth, giving it away freely and with passion. Such generosity will come back to bless you forever. As the ghost of Marley passionately declaimed to Ebenezer Scrooge in Charles Dickens' *A Christmas Carol*, "Business! Mankind was my business! The common welfare was my business! The dealings of my trade were but a drop of water in the comprehensive ocean of my business!"

Although many people in our culture are beginning to question the assumptions of the American dream, we still live in a time of compulsive and wasteful consumerism. Per capita consumption in the United States has increased 45 percent in the past twenty years. During the same period, quality of life as measured by the index of social health has *decreased* by roughly the same percentage.[2] The average working woman plays with her children forty minutes a week — and shops six hours.[3] Ninety-three percent of teenage girls list shopping as their favorite pastime.[4]

No one is immune to the cultural misconceptions about the value of money, including those we turn to for help. Many therapists have little knowledge of the problems of affluenza beyond a rudimentary understanding of workaholism and compulsive spending or gambling. Both client and therapist sit facing each other equally sold on the myth of the American dream and trying to solve a problem that neither one recognizes. In addition, some therapists feel little sympathy for the rich person. Like anyone else, they can be intimidated, envious, or just plain distracted by the external trappings of wealth, and fail to see the human being beneath the flashy "package." For those in the top 1 percent of personal income, it can be more lonely and difficult to get help than one might think.

The following are some tools, strategies, and new theories that I have found helpful and effective in my work with clients and their families suffering from affluenza. They comprise the essence of the therapeutic program I utilize in treating this condition.

Preventive Medicine: Immunizing the Children

DEMYSTIFY THE WEALTH TABOO

"The most important thing parents can communicate is that all questions are fine. Given our culture's taboo about discussing money, many of us can't talk about it comfortably, so I say talking about it uncomfortably is fine," says John Levy, a consultant for individuals and families on issues of inheritance.[5] How the inhabitants of the golden ghetto handle their wealth both emotionally and practically depends, to a great degree, on how they were raised. Telling children early whether they will inherit their parents' fortune makes for a good start. Answering their questions truthfully and at the appropriate age is another way to take the mystery out of the situation.

Unfortunately, many parents keep their children in the dark about their inheritance. This is a powerful and demeaning way to control their behavior, although certainly not all parents have that motive. Many are simply trying to protect their children from what they consider a burdensome responsibility. Some follow the doctrine of "You just don't talk about those things" or "What they don't know won't hurt them." The truth is that what they don't know *will* hurt them—and possibly irreversibly. The lessons needed to handle wealth in a healthy way are many and bear repeating, so it is best to begin early. How early? As soon as the children start asking questions. As with questions about sex and procreation, the explanation can be tailored to the developmental level of the child. Levy continues, "When a small child asks, 'Are we rich?,' the real question often is, 'Are we safe?'" What they really want to know is that there is enough money to take care of their basic survival needs. As their need for more information grows, so will their questions. As with any other important part of their lives, it is our job as responsible parents not to overload or over-whelm them with extraneous information that they may not un-derstand. Children—and adults!—can only process so many facts and figures at one time. Unlike adults, however, children are re-markably adept at letting us know when enough is enough.

As they begin to feel safe, and their curiosity grows, they will begin to want to know how much money is available and for what. At this point in a child's development, it is time to begin to instill your family or individual moral beliefs and mores about wealth and its use for the world at large. How much is "enough" to keep for your own security and how much are you willing to share with others? What is a necessity and what is not?

Editors Anne Slepian and Christopher Mogil of *More Than Money*, a quarterly newsletter that explores the personal, political and social justice aspects of wealth, summarize the ways con-cerned parents have addressed the issue of how to ensure that their well-intentioned gifts of inheritance don't undermine their children's motivation, self-confidence, or relationships.

1. Model a healthy attitude toward work, and help school-age and teenage children try out a variety of money-making and volunteer work experiences.
2. Accept that young adults may have long periods of work exploration, given the expanded options that money brings. Give plenty of encouragement and guidance (not pressure) to young people trying to find their way.
3. Distinguish between the value of meaningful engagement (work) and the value of earning money (knowing one can support oneself), and help young adults do the same.
4. Handle your own money well—spending, saving, and giving.
5. Teach children financial competence, starting young, as part of regular family life. As age appropriate, let children know ahead what money they can expect, when, and why.
6. Give teens and young adults gradually increasing amounts to manage, so that by the time trust funds come they have practiced with sizable sums. Let them learn from their own choices and mistakes.
7. Let teenagers stand on their own merits and make their own mistakes, and don't use money to bail them out or open doors for them.
8. Encourage young adults to take risks and sustain their efforts in the face of challenges—not just move on when situations get difficult because their money provides that freedom.
9. Help young people find respectful mentors who can help them use money well—not as an escape, but as a tool toward something meaningful.
10. Have close friends who are not wealthy; raise children

where they make friends with a mix of people; encourage contact (e.g., through volunteering) across class lines.

11. Communicate with young adults about money issues such as resentment, envy, trust, being open about money or not, making loans and gifts, power differences, and dependence. Acknowledge that even a small trust fund makes their financial life quite different from peers who have no such cushion.

12. Teach children the ways that money and class can create differences between people (e.g., people will have different expectations of what their lives will be like) but that having wealth does not make people better or worse than others. Show them ways they can act out of concern for injustice, rather than guilt for their advantages.[6]

Although it is important to keep the discussion about one's financial affairs open and honest throughout our lives, it is particularly important to make your intentions known and understood by all potential heirs as old age approaches. If the lines of communication have been open all along, the final discussions will be simply an extension of one's lifelong practice of integrity. For those who have avoided the subject, this discussion of a will or trust can be a jarring acknowledgment of death. However, psychologically, it is an important part of the acceptance process for both the parent and the child. For my father, it seemed to bring a sort of peace knowing that I understood and accepted his disbursement decisions and his reasons for them. I have always felt strongly that it was his money and that he could do anything he wanted to with it. Having separated the money from the love some time ago, I knew that the amount he did or did not leave me in no way reflected the love he felt for me.

Again, the discussion should not be a onetime event. Children understand different concepts at different stages of their development, so it is important to keep the conversation open and free-flowing. It is also a good idea to keep children up-to-date about a new will, trust, lawyer, or accountant. The future emotional health of the inheritor relies heavily on his or her ability to understand the feelings and reasoning behind the financial planning of the parent.

TAKE THE EMPHASIS OFF EXTERNALS

Validation is necessary for the healthy development of any child's self-esteem. Yet this is sometimes neglected in the world of affluent youngsters, who are quite often surrounded by a culture that places great value on names, external appearances, and high (or higher) achievement. Because these children are expected to live up to their name or heritage, it is particularly important that they be affirmed and validated for who *they* are, not the "important family" from which they come.

I try to caution wealthy parents about the harm of being vicariously ambitious for their children and overly concerned with externals. This attitude often causes children to become joyless overachievers, who are unable to savor their accomplishments and "burn out" at a very early age. When one is a parent, it is often difficult to know where to draw the line between encouragement and proper restraint. We all enjoy seeing our children excel, and when one has the financial resources to buy the tools or training to help them, it is easy to get caught up in providing children with endless opportunities to achieve. The danger in this kind of "help" is that the children may begin to feel that they are loved only for what they do. When they become adults, they may be driven to more and more audacious exploits in an attempt to court approval and love. (Another danger is that they will move aimlessly from one activity to another—and miss the experience of being a child!)

These children may also hold on to their childhood success as the measuring stick for any future endeavors—forever falling short of their previous level of unhealthy perfectionism. The flip side of trying to do something perfectly is to not attempt to do it at all. To risk failure in our perfectionistic society is to risk shame. Innumerable societal dictums set us all up to fail in our own eyes and in the eyes of others. "A task worth doing is worth doing well." The entire world of competitive sports is a giant arena for perfectionism; for someone to win, there must be a loser. The very word *loser* brings shame to anyone who carries that label.

It is of paramount importance that the home environment be accepting, nonjudgmental, uncritical, and supportive of each child's uniqueness and special contributions to the family. As all children do, children of affluence will undoubtedly compare and contrast themselves to their peers—in this case, to other children in the wealthy community—and will often find themselves lacking. In adolescents, this emphasis on externals often further weakens their shaky, volatile self-esteem and self-confidence.

The tendency to define one's self-worth in material terms— designer label clothes, elite vacation spots, expensive cars—is greater and more alluring in the wealthy world. This is true in part because these things are more available to the rich. And quite simply, the children want them. As parents, it is natural to want to please our children and far more difficult to say "no" and explain *why* we are saying no when our children know we can afford to buy them whatever they want. This pressure is increased when the next-door neighbors give in to their child's every whim and your children have discovered the manipulative art of constantly comparing you to them.

In spite of the urge to indulge our children, as concerned, emotionally healthy parents, we must seize every opportunity to model appropriate, self-esteem-building behavior, which is a true reflection of our internal values. In any household, rich or poor, this frequently means saying "no." By staying in touch with our own feelings and mirroring our children's, we will create an environment conducive to honest and ongoing communication. By focusing on our own internal virtues and expressing them clearly, we will encourage our children to do the same. Children are more likely to internalize these positive lessons if they truly believe we are presenting them with an accurate account of who we are. Children, particularly teenagers, can spot a hypocrite a mile away. In Twelve Step lingo, you must not only "talk the talk," you must also "walk the walk."

DISMANTLE THE FALSE SENSE OF ENTITLEMENT

As previously discussed, many wealthy children grow up with a distorted sense of their importance in the world; they view themselves as special and deserving. They often behave erratically, vacillating between false, obnoxious bravado and uncomfortable shyness. Feeling alienated and different, they may be nervous and unsure how to relate to the person of average means. The image they project is seldom a true reflection of the child within. Because they have not received the mirroring and nurturing that would foster a strong sense of self, they tend to rely heavily on externals to tell them and others who they are—where they fit in the "real" world.

Parents, therapists, or significant others of wealthy people can gently help them to dismantle their false sense of entitlement. We are all special, unique, and different. Encourage them to discover *how* they are special, beyond the mere fact of their personal or family wealth. Given the power of money, their narcissism may very well be the only yardstick by which they've defined themselves. Remember that feeling entitled can lead to personality traits that are difficult to tolerate. In adults, there are frequently accompanying addictions to deal with. The greatest gift you can give them and yourself is to first *accept* them the way they are. Acceptance creates a nurturing space in which change can begin to unfold.

LEARN TO DELAY GRATIFICATION
AND TOLERATE FRUSTRATION

As illustrated in chapter 4, wealthy children are frequently materially satiated at the same time that they are emotionally deprived. They can have any object they want, but they still feel empty inside. Such experiences often produce adults who have an inability to delay gratification—they are impatient and demanding when their material desires are not immediately satisfied as they were in childhood. People who grow up with this distorted understanding of the world are not prepared for a life that will include the frustrations inherent in self-discipline, achievement, and ongoing deep relationships. Often they are depressed and alienated because they feel superfluous. All essential goods and services are bought for them; they are not even expected to do simple household tasks. Because of this, these children miss out on the opportunity to feel needed and important within the family structure, and lose many opportunities to develop healthy self-esteem. They are simply "ornaments on the family tree, and they know it."[7]

As adults, the very fact that their material desires are instantly fulfilled causes them to experience "gratification" differently than people of average means. Nonaffluent people must usually work for and plan how they will be gratified, what material goods or services they will use their money to buy. Thus, there is constant pressure exerted on them by their circumstances to make their selections conscious ones that are truly desired or needed. Wealthy people, on the other hand, can buy almost anything they want. They don't have to weigh the benefits of one selection against that of another. They can have it all—but not really. Gratification also involves a subtle feeling of being rewarded, of tasting the sweetness of one's own labors. Whereas nonaffluent people are theoretically trading their work for that of another when they buy something, wealthy people are not always giving of themselves for a purchase. They often subconsciously suspect that they are not holding up their end of the bargain.

It is important that children be given age-appropriate responsibilities within the household. This will help them feel valued, integral, and necessary to the family, and their self-esteem and self-worth will grow accordingly. It's important for all of us to feel needed. We want to know that what we do matters to someone. Following quickly on the heels of the inheritance from my mother, I realized that I no longer needed to exert any noticeable control over my spending. Along with this loss of parameters came the loss of one of the only two people who really cared what I did or didn't do. Going through my first divorce, an only child with one remaining alcoholic parent, my sole daily responsibility was to feed my two dogs. I felt a new terror in knowing that nothing I did really affected anyone. My actions were useless. They served no greater purpose than to please myself in the moment—an understanding that rapidly led to acts of self-destruction.

Parents also need to allow their children to feel the consequences of their behavior; don't buy their way out of their mistakes. Being held accountable for one's actions is an important step toward learning what the acceptable boundaries are within our society. We must allow our children to experience healthy frustration from time to time. If we can say "no" to some of their material requests—not because we can't afford what they want but because we love them and have their best interests at heart— we can teach them to tolerate frustration and delay gratification.

This low tolerance for frustration is one of the most disabling characteristics of children and adult children of dysfunctional affluent homes. Because I normally don't *have* to do whatever it is that I'm doing, if it becomes the least bit boring or frustrating, I can simply walk away. Where nonaffluent people consciously or unconsciously rely on external motivators such as the need to earn a living to keep them on task, wealthy people must use self-discipline. They must somehow create their own structure within a space devoid of any normal parameters. This behavior may or may not have been modeled in their family of origin.

This is the most difficult task for many of my clients—to decide what they want to do, what their mission in life is. Faced with the financial possibility of doing anything they want, they are frequently terrified to try anything at all. One client, Mary, knows many things she *does not* want to do or be. But when we discuss some things that she might want to do with her life, she self-sabotages by saying that she is not rich enough to do what she *really* wants to do (in Mary's case, owning a large, independent bookstore). Her inability to produce the capital to start such a store would expose her in the world of wealth as a fraud, she feels, and yet she is wealthy enough that she can afford not to take an everyday, nine-to-five job. Deeply dissatisfied with her loneliness and isolation, and aware of her self-sabotaging, Mary has begun to venture out into new activities in the "ordinary" world. These experiences are teaching her to judge others not by the dictates of her past, which tell her that these people are socially or economically "beneath" her, but for how they fit into and contribute to her life now. Long worried about and obsessed by the need to decide what she wants to do with her life, Mary is beginning to see that it is the actual "living" of her life that will lead her to what she really wants. She is learning, in other words, to follow her heart.

There is a great deal of attention being given to a new measurement of future success called *emotional intelligence.* In his best-selling book by that name, author Daniel Goleman writes that a study of the impulse control of four-year-olds showed that those who could "restrain their emotions and so delay impulse" were, as adolescents, "more socially competent: personally effective, self-assertive, and better able to cope with the frustrations of life. They were less likely to . . . become rattled and disorganized when pressured; they embraced challenges and pursued them instead of giving up even in the face of difficulties; they were self-reliant, trustworthy, and dependable; they took the initiative. . . ." Furthermore, Goleman notes that "the ability to delay gratification contributes powerfully to intellectual potential."[8] Yet children of affluence, who are expected to be high achievers, are often sorely lacking in the very skills that foretell future emotional and intellectual success. Ironically, it is the substance of highest value in our society, money, that creates this predisposition to doom.

The good news about emotional intelligence is that "there is ample evidence that emotional skills such as impulse control . . . *can* be learned."[9] We can help our children and ourselves learn these skills. The earlier children develop these skills, the better. It is much harder to learn how to be patient when you are forty than when you are four.

I have always particularly disliked the derogatory label "spoiled brat." It makes me think of a piece of fruit, not a child. It suggests no hope for improvement. I have never seen anything "spoiled" get better. I *have* seen many children of affluence learn to tolerate frustration and delay gratification. Poor impulse control can be reversed. Patience can be learned. Even as adults, with enough awareness and enough guidance we can learn to do things differently.

I have a client named Ellen who has struggled repeatedly with her inability to finish writing a book she started years ago. She has had similar difficulty sticking with the different jobs she's taken during the three years we've been working together. Ellen has two separate issues she is battling. The first is an inability to tolerate frustration.

Second, she is sometimes trapped by her black-and-white, all-or-nothing thinking pattern that originated in her early childhood. As a young child, she was literally and figuratively locked in a wire mesh cage (her mother's idea of a playpen; it was similar to a chicken coop), watching from afar as her mother lived the seemingly carefree life of a frivolous, charming, beautiful socialite. As

Ellen grew older, she was no longer locked in her cage, but her life was as closed off as ever. She had no friends and spent a good deal of time in her room, often alone. Helpless, she watched her mother's life whirl faster and faster, entertaining a constant stream of lovers and friends, until her mother ultimately committed suicide.

For Ellen, the horrible irony is that the life her mother led had looked far better and much more desirable than her own sad and lonely existence. With one anguished act of self-destruction, however, her mother shattered her daughter's illusion and turned the yearned-for dream into a nightmare. Ellen was seventeen when her mother died. Like many children from dysfunctional families, Ellen lacked healthy role models. She felt she had to choose between the lesser of two evils: a child's life filled with isolation, depression, and loneliness, or the gaiety of the socialite with the accompanying fear that this life led to certain death.

As an adult in recovery from affluenza, Ellen is beginning to dismantle the myth and to focus a healthy anger toward the old patterns that have been controlling her life. She is starting to see that she *can* and *wants* to live in the gray area—somewhere between black and white—even though learning to do so is frustrating and difficult at times. She knows now that she has choices, and that one option is to take some of her mother's qualities and make them her own—and *not* die. Another option is to write her book, which requires her to be isolated at times, but not necessarily lonely and depressed.

Ellen has learned that she can break up her day into periods of intense work and social activity. I have suggested that she continue her struggle to separate the present from the past, bearing as much of the frustration of feeling "caged" as she can when she is writing, taking a break to be with people, and then going back and writing some more. Slowly, she will begin to create her own reality around her behavior. She will no longer be operating from an all-

or-nothing state of mind, blindly reacting to old stimuli. Hopefully, her anger at the repetition of old patterns will give her some of the energy necessary to break free.

At the very least, Ellen's anger is now focused outside of herself, which has partially alleviated her depression. She has learned not to be angry at *herself* for not being able to write or stick with a job. She understands her push-pull relationship with the artificial, affluent lifestyle that her mother led, and she has the awareness and determination to break the destructive cycle of affluenza that has destroyed so much of her family.

Often, recovery from affluenza requires learning to tolerate the frustration and discomfort inherent in doing something a new way—a better, healthier way. A person can delay the gratification of feeling better right now, which usually means reverting to old behaviors, and choose to wait for the greater rewards of increasing self-respect and self-esteem that comes from growth and change. I always remind my clients that change is a continuing process. There is no ultimate "there" for us to get to and stop. The process of change and growth is the only "there" we will ever know. After a life of solitude where she was restrained, separated, and "cushioned" by affluence from the dynamic flux of life, Ellen is finally growing up and learning, not because she has to, but because she wants to.

Another difficulty that people like Ellen experience is the need to be in control. As discussed earlier, this desire usually stems directly from emotional deprivation during childhood, which drives us to control others out of fear that, if we don't, our emotional needs will certainly go unmet once again. Along with intolerance for frustration and the inability to delay gratification, the need to control produces self-sabotaging behaviors that are insidious, persistent, and difficult to alter. For example, in the initial stages of a relationship, there is an extended time of exploration and uncertainty. A mature, emotionally healthy adult has the patience for and actually looks forward to the give and take involved in establishing the boundaries or parameters of the relationship. An emotionally deprived child will most likely become an adult who, upon entering a potentially intimate relationship, will begin to operate from a place of neediness, or lack—an emotional state that reflects the childhood deprivation. Out of fear of abandonment and deprivation, the adult will try to control the situation, prematurely forcing the relationship to fit his or her expectations. In this process, the individual often loses the very thing he or she was trying to hang on to; the relationship ends and the abandonment and deprivation are reinforced.

DIFFUSE AFFLUENT CULTURAL AND FAMILY EXPECTATIONS

Unfortunately, many wealthy families go to great lengths to protect their empires, and "weak links" are simply not allowed. Shy children, who in a nonaffluent home might be allowed to be themselves, are sometimes ostracized in affluent homes because they are not what their parents need to carry on the family business. Within affluent families, there are strong cultural sanctions, spoken and unspoken, that dictate what constitutes an "acceptable" personality for the rich child. Only the strongest survive. Little nurturing or time is given to those who stumble along the way.

Being born into a dynasty, the male children in particular are required to assume a mantle of power and control. Ironically, the emotionally deprived and dysfunctional upbringing many of these children experience often causes them to fall far short of their families' expectations.When these children grow up to be self-destructive, their families go to great extremes and expense to cover up their "weaknesses" and bail them out of trouble. Other children are simply not emotionally or intellectually capable of following in the footsteps of the Family Founder—often very large footsteps, indeed. These "substandard" children are quietly sent away, usually after being bought off, and left to their own devices as long as their behavior does not jeopardize the family fortune or reputation.

It doesn't take long for young children growing up in wealthy families to figure out what the expectations are for them. They experience much fear and frequently rebel as they await the final verdict on their suitability to move into the foreground of the family empire. If a young person fails to measure up, he or she faces not only the repercussions from within the family itself, but sometimes derisive media attention as well.

Following a recent family wedding, I spent a delightful afternoon with one of my cousins, George Wilson, and his family. Talking to him, I realized that growing up as a Wilson, one of the preeminent Detroit families, gave him an entirely different perspective than I had experienced growing up in Delray Beach, Florida, as a Hoyle—my mother's married name. The power and mystique that the Wilson family name held, in addition to living in Detroit, made it impossible for many of the second and even third generation to find their own identities. Even if they did, others found it impossible to see around their name to the person beneath. George and many of my other cousins, particularly the men who carried the last name, left Detroit so they could live anonymously. Some even found it necessary to rid themselves of their inherited money so that they could prove—to themselves and perhaps to others— that they could make it on their own. It is interesting to observe that, once secure in their own right and identity, many of my family members have returned "home" to the Detroit area.

It is our job as parents and therapists to diffuse the destructive and dehumanizing expectations that have been passed on consciously and unconsciously to the children of affluence. With love, our time, and nurturance we can make all children feel needed and wanted.

ALLOW MAXIMUM FREEDOM IN CHOICE OF CAREER

Many parents who have acquired wealth on their own, or at least substantially bolstered the family fortune, have also acquired a sense of personal power. They are sometimes overzealous in their desire to "help" their offspring, which translates into directing their lives. They often keep their children in the family business or bankroll any of their new ventures in order to maintain control over them. Wise parents, however, resist this urge and allow their children maximum freedom in their choice of career. Some children will feel an intense need to establish their independence, others will not. Most of us, regardless of age or financial position, respond far better to encouragement combined with a sense of personal choice, than to parental or exterior control.

Wealthy people often carry a vague sense of guilt, as though they don't deserve to be so "lucky." Children who are allowed to go out and succeed on their own are, in a sense, proving that they do deserve their good fortune, that they are worthy. For some, a career outside the family business is important simply for the pleasure that accomplishment can bring. After experimentation and trial and error, many children of wealthy parents do come home to the family business; but it builds their self-esteem and character to know that they can make it on their own first. Still others see staying in the family business as an opportunity and a responsibility. They have been given a chance to perpetuate a successful enterprise and share that largesse with other family members and society in general.

SEPARATING MONEY AND LOVE

Where exactly is the money complex hidden? Most often it hides in the guises of love, where so much soul is always hidden. . . . Giving, receiving, saving, participating, supporting, spending, willing (inheritance) are the ways one learns about loving. . . . To

> Protestant-capitalist consciousness [renouncing] the family's psychological attitudes often becomes refusing money from home which is felt at home as a rebuff of love.[10]

Those of us who are children of affluent parents are all too aware of the inclination within our culture to regard the gift of money as an expression of feeling. Money becomes, in many ways and within many families, a substitute for love. The results of this substitution are all too apparent in the enormous amount of dysfunctional behavior within the so-called privileged class. On the other hand, to receive a generous inheritance from someone who has honestly loved you and cared for you, or to leave money to someone you have loved, is a genuine and generous expression of caring.

Unfortunately, it may be the only thing one ever receives from a parent who invested little time or love in the relationship. Commenting on the pain inherent in such parent-child relationships, a friend of mine remarked, "You may not have made the money yourself, but you've certainly earned it." Likewise, some parents may feel that their gifts of money are true expressions of their love. An acquaintance related the story of his brother-in-law, Bob, who is a member of a prominent New England family which can trace their ancestry to the Mayflower and Governor Bradford. The family made its fortune in the maritime China trade several generations back, and the money continues to be passed down from generation to generation. As children, Bob and his younger brother would come down the stairs every Christmas morning to find, at the bottom step, a sterling silver Paul Revere bowl that held two checks for $100 each. That was the extent of Christmas morning for them. Their parents were invariably not at home, having already left for the day to engage in the ritual round of high-society holiday socializing. To this day, Bob will have nothing to do with Christmas; decorations or celebrating of any kind associated with the holiday are banned from his household. Although he earned a degree from an Ivy League college, Bob has never worked and for many years has declined to participate in the world in any way; he rarely leaves the house and refuses to answer or talk on the phone.

There is often a thin line to walk between money and love, and parents or potential bestowers of the wealth need to understand the perils involved. The heir will feel that the inheritance is a more genuine act of love if it is obvious that the parent put time and thought into the selection and timing of the distributions, whether cash or material possessions.

My Aunt Betty died of breast cancer several years ago. She was the most influential female mentor in my life. Some time before her death we had discussed her plans, and she had explained that she was leaving me no money since she knew my parents would take care of that. I understood completely and nothing was ever mentioned again.

In the months before her death, I made several trips to Florida to spend as much time with her as possible. Knowing how much I admired and enjoyed driving her 1986 white Jaguar, she kindly offered to let me use it on each of my visits. A few days before she died, she handed me the title for the Jaguar and said she would like me to have it. To this day, I cry when I think of the kindness and love that went into that gift. It was apparent to me and all the other inheritors that she had put much time and consideration into each gift. Each one was carefully matched to the receiver. Her love for each of us was as immense and real after her death as it had been before.

Nothing can replace the combination of love and careful consideration and planning when passing our wealth from generation to generation. It is truly a gift when we can give our children not only money but the wisdom with which to use it. This is beautifully illustrated in the following letter from Arthur Davidson, the secretary and cofounder of Harley-Davidson Motor Co., written to his son Arthur on his thirty-fifth birthday.

HARLEY-DAVIDSON MOTOR CO.

MOTORCYCLES   SERVI-CARS   AND   PACKAGE   TRUCKS

MILWAUKEE 1, WIS., U. S. A.

WM. H. DAVIDSON, PRES. AND GERL. MGR.
GORDON M. DAVIDSON, VICE PRESIDENT
WM. J. HARLEY, TREASURER AND CHIEF ENGINEER
ARTHUR DAVIDSON, SECY. AND GENL. SALES MGR.

CABLE ADDRESS "HARDAVMOCY"
CODES: { LIEBER'S WESTERN UNION
A.B.C. 4TH & 5TH EDITIONS
BENTLEY'S AND
A.B.C. 5TH IMPROVED.

April 6, 1949

Mr. Arthur H. Davidson
c/o Remuda Ranch
Wickenburg, Arizona

Dear Arthur:

        A long time ago I wrote you a birthday card to be delivered
on your 35th birthday. Many things have happened since, but the birthday card was always accumulating, and now it is yours. I know it will
be well handled and you will do good with it. You are receiving it at
an age when it will do you the most good, and it puts you and your
family in a position to enjoy the things in life that money can buy.
But the real enjoyment out of life you will find is doing for others
who maybe are not quite as fortunate.

        Am not preaching a sermon, Arthur, just trying to tell you
how to get the most good out of this birthday card, which is now yours.

        Can't make this a letter to both you and Janet because I am
writing about your Trust Fund and your 35th birthday, but I know you
will both enjoy it, take good care of it, use it wisely, and be generous. Remember, you and Janet set the standards of your house.

        Your mother and I are mighty glad to be able to sign the
agreement turning over to you the balance that is in your Trust Fund.

        Well, Arthur, maybe I sound a little sentimental today, but
I am mighty proud to be able to have this birthday card come out as
well as it did, and I know you can't blame mother and me for being
just a bit sentimental on your 35th birthday.

        Again I say, enjoy your money, use your talents wisely, and
be charitable to others.

                        Your

                        Dad.

A balanced relationship with wealth can afford one the time and means to pursue true love; love of ourselves, of God in ourselves, and the love of others. As I take a deep breath and turn slowly around to look at my life, I realize that with my affluence I support and nurture the lives of many people whom I love deeply. That knowledge gives me immense satisfaction and pleasure.

WHEN PARENTS ARE UNABLE TO PARENT

Children who have the most motivation are generally those who feel very loved. When parents are emotionally or physically unavailable, the right mentor, surrogate parent, or therapist can sometimes help to fill the gap. Finding someone to stand in for my parents was the saving grace of my life. My aunt Betty Hunt and my first mother-in-law, Betty Baker, were strong, positive role models for me. They showed me that there was another way of being: a healthy, loving, productive way to live one's life, without self-pity and grandiosity. My "uncle" Baxter Taylor, my father's oldest and best friend, has shown me that a man can be there for me consistently and with unconditional love. I am deeply grateful for their presence in my life. For those of you whose lives might touch an emotionally isolated, abandoned child, affluent or not, know that you can make a huge difference in the quality of that child's life.

Only nurturing and time can truly teach people that they are lovable, worthwhile, and capable of making a healthy, intelligent decision about the future. As parents, it is our job to support our children in their personal journey of discovering who they really are and what their interests and dreams are. We must help them to find their heart's desire and support them while they follow it. People do their best at the work they love.

Whether we're therapists or parents, the most powerful tool at our disposal is love. If we show our children that we care about the choices they make, we will go a long way toward improving the quality of their journey. In reflecting how we see their behaviors and choices affect them, and by taking the time to help them define their goals and develop plans to reach them, we are showing them that they matter, to us and to the larger world. Using healthy tools of parenting—such as holding reasonable expectations, using loving, firm discipline, allowing children to experience the consequences of their behavior, role modeling healthy boundaries in intimate relationships as well as setting them with our children—are important for all parents, rich or poor. In addition, affluent parents must be conscious of their own behaviors and beliefs around the handling of money and the messages about money that they are consciously and unconsciously passing on to their children. Clear, open, and honest communication around the family fortune, as mentioned before, is very important. By taking that precious time, showing your love, and having faith and confidence in your child's abilities, you have given him or her the irreplaceable gift of growth, positive self-esteem, and self-love.

*   *   *   *

The freedom of my wealth, which I once viewed as "awful," has become a wonderful gift, and the "endless possibilities" have become tangible, reachable goals. With each door that is opened, I now see a new room full of entrances and exits, and I can hardly wait to try each one. Sometimes the choices wealth allows me are still overwhelming and terrifying. When these feelings find me, I take a step back and remember that within me and within us all is the knowledge, the intuition, and the spiritual guidance to make any decision that is necessary. With time and patience, terrifying choices begin to look more and more like challenges and opportunities.

Tools for Healing

My expertise as a therapist is threefold and comes from several different sources. I am both personally and professionally trained in the fields of addiction, codependency, experiential therapy and psychodrama. During my years of recovery from various addictions and codependency, I have used all the tools described in the remainder of this chapter with success. Professionally, I have encouraged clients to use many of these same tools and have watched with immense satisfaction as their healing unfolded. I find that I work most effectively with clients whose problems I have experienced, and I teach most effectively those tools of recovery that have most helped me. The problems that I, my clients, and many of my friends have encountered and to which these tools have been effectively applied include the following: affluenza, acute substance addiction and abuse, codependency, and other maladaptive behaviors resulting from being an adult child of a dysfunctional home. In my practice, I have treated individual adults, couples, and adolescents and have used these methods successfully with all these populations. The presenting symptoms of my clients are frequently depression, anxiety, low self-esteem, lack of confidence and direction in life resulting in loss of identity, and spiritual, if not financial bankruptcy. In Twelve Step lingo, they have "bottomed out."

FINDING THE RIGHT THERAPIST

In my experience, it has been very difficult to understand what role money has in my life — what it allows me to do, who it allows me to be, and how it "dictates" my being. There is no point, regardless of the level of affluence, where one ceases to struggle with these fundamental issues. People experience something of the possibility of change within themselves when in the grips of the transformational power of money. For many people, rich or not, money has become the talisman of the self. By this I mean, the way in which we use our money, the expression of wealth in our lives, becomes who we are.

If one has been raised in a dysfunctional affluent home, that sense of self, that feeling of high esteem that comes from knowing one is valued and makes a difference in the world, is difficult to attain. Recovering that self often requires the assistance of a therapist well versed in the uniqueness and subtleties of the affluent world; one who is at least aware that there are differences between an adult or child of a nonwealthy dysfunctional home and someone who has wealth-related problems. It is particularly important to find a therapist who has no prejudice against the rich. Trust your intuition; if you're wealthy, you've lived with the prejudice all your life and you can certainly identify it. When interviewing potential counselors, it is important to ask questions such as, "Do you feel that affluent people have any problems that might be unique to their class? If so, what are they?" Don't give up and don't settle for less than you deserve—a therapist who cares about your well-being, not because of what you have or the fact that you can afford to pay your bill, but because of who you are.

A competent therapist along with a number of therapeutic tools which you can use on your own can help you uncover your covert beliefs and enable you to make financial and wealth-related decisions from a conscious place. Journaling or letter writing, emotional release exercises, creative visualization combined with meditation, and nondefensive and nonoffensive communication can all help in taking the unhealthy emotional charge out of your financial relationship with your partner, your children, and society at large. In the following section, we will briefly explore each of these tools.

CREATE STRUCTURE, MOTIVATION, PURPOSE AND MISSION

As discussed earlier, the endless spectrum of choices and possibilities available to the affluent often become psychologically overwhelming and unmanageable. On the other hand, some affluent people feel compelled to put themselves at risk or to undertake extraordinary challenges because their daily lives are terminally comfortable, often devoid of the risk inherent in the fight to survive. Searching for ways to prove to themselves that they are alive and breathing, they leap from one experience to the next, often reaching the extremes of negative and irresponsible behavior. We see these extremes glorified or belittled by the media on a daily basis: drug and alcohol abuse, marital infidelities and multiple marriages, giant business mergers, heroic and dangerous athletic accomplishments, and lavish parties.

One of the positive aspects of wealth is that it does, in fact, afford one freedom from the day-to-day problems of survival. When a group of college students were asked how they thought money would change their lives, they repeatedly used the word *freedom*. They would have freedom to do what they wanted, go where they pleased, and certainly freedom from having to work.[11] At some point, however, the wealthy usually come to realize that the freedom money purchases is, in many ways, false. Wealth brings an independence fraught with so many perilous choices that the money often becomes a nightmare rather than a dream come true.

How many of us have dreamed of winning the lottery? A woman in Colorado who won $6.85 million reports, "One sister didn't speak to us for a year, because we didn't pick up a breakfast check; another expected us to repay her school loans. A close friend borrowed money and we didn't hear from him again for three years—when he called to borrow some more."[12]

And she had better hope that she doesn't die before the final installment is paid! (Most lottery jackpots are paid out over a twenty-year period.) An analysis by the North American Association of State and Provincial Lotteries quoted in a *New York Times Magazine* article on Lotto winners states, "'What can happen to a deceased lottery winner's estate and beneficiaries? Answer: A financial disaster of incredible proportion." The analysis describes the tax liability for the heirs of an unmarried winner of a twenty-million dollar jackpot—payable in annual installments of one million dollars over twenty years—who dies after receiving the first payment. The heirs would receive a tax bill of more than five million.[13]

Furthermore, that tax bill is due right away, long before the money arrives. "Estate taxes—on the unpaid total—are payable immediately, with monthly penalties added, after nine months. Even if the heirs have no cash. Even if there's nothing in the late winner's estate except those great expectations. The heirs owe taxes on every million they thought their rich uncle had left to them."[14]

Just as what looks like a gift can, in fact, be an incredible burden, so can having an endless array of possibilities be paralyzing. What appears to be freedom to the nonaffluent person can in reality be a yawning abyss, too terrifying for the affluent individual to contemplate on his or her own. In many ways, an individual with money lives in a virtual prison, frozen in fear; in fact, many wealthy people have said that they felt imprisoned by their wealth. This reality is the very opposite of how the less affluent perceive the rich. Though many people in our culture equate wealth with freedom, the truth is that psychologically, prison walls can be constructed of infinite possibilities as well as a severe limitation of choices. The message I share with my clients is that, beyond the assurance of survival needs (food, clothing, and shelter), true freedom comes only from a profound inner sense of security and well-being.

TRUST AND SHARE

The way we share our fortunes is closely connected to our ability to trust. Whether we perceive our money as an overwhelming burden or a bountiful gift is profoundly revealed in our attitude toward trust. Not surprisingly, the secret to living with money in a healthy way seems to be in the sharing of the good fortune. Among all of the wealthy people I interviewed, those who have been able to participate personally in the sharing of their wealth have been the ones who have experienced the greatest pleasure. They seem to be the most comfortable with their abundance and there is a sense of acceptance, expansion, and ease about them.

One young heir had found a creative, healthy, fun way to share his money with his friends and employees. His employees all owned part of his company, so when the business profited, they did too. He built a huge ranch that was open to his employees and friends, and he spent most of his weekends there. He trusted his judgment of people and was not concerned, as many wealthy people are, that others might be taking advantage of him. So, unlike many affluent people, he was far from isolated. Surrounded by happy people, he had the satisfying knowledge that he had contributed greatly to their happiness.

This past Christmas, shortly before my father died, he and I decided to give a gift to each of his "angels," the wonderful, caring women who took care of him in his final days. When I went to visit him in North Carolina, they had only been with him a short time, but they had already shown him such love and compassion that I felt certain my father would be well nurtured and cared for when I had to leave. I learned a valuable and unforgettable lesson that weekend. The joy that I received from their gratitude for our gift was incredible. Perhaps that is God's reward to us, to nudge us in the direction of more sharing and giving. In spite of my sorrow that my father was ailing, I left his side feeling renewed, revitalized, and reconnected to God. Giving of ourselves and our abundance will be discussed in greater depth in the next chapter.

"COMING OUT" AS WEALTHY

I think it is important that we, as wealthy adults, own who we are. It's time we stopped hiding and being ashamed of our money. This whole "coming out" process has been a fascinating and enlightening side effect of my work with affluenza. I have begun to realize that, although my wealth is by no means all that I am, it is a very important part of me. By acknowledging the presence of money and its effects on my life, I have become more and more comfortable with it.

Learning to be comfortable with wealth is often a long and arduous process. My friend Robin Kyle told me that she was depressed for days following our interview. Here I was, she observed, asking her about all the things in her life that she tries not to think about. By directly confronting her with these issues, I was forcing her to take an honest look at her feelings about being rich. Learning to accept the realities of our lives has important and long-lasting benefits. If someone tries to give you something, tangible or not, that you refuse to accept and keep fending off, you will have little time to do anything else and certainly little control over the situation. If you accept it, whatever "it" might be, and make it part of you, then you can *do anything you want* with it. If we allow our wealth to become a part of who we are, then it no longer controls our behavior and we can get on with our lives.

DISPEL THE ILLUSION OF CONTROL

In contrast to the sixties and seventies, when freedom and emancipation were the rule, the eighties and nineties have been about a search for control. This can be attributed partially to the upheavals, failures, and disillusionment the past two decades have brought with them: terrorism, AIDS, moral chaos, religious cults, soul-destroying materialism, the spread of poverty, massive drug use, and the decline of the American educational system coupled with a feeling that we are failing our children.

The creation and expansion of wealth are expressions of the urge to be in control. Having money can create the fantasy of being in control of one's life and destiny, but this is only an illusion. The accumulation of money or power does not provide real security. As we have seen, as wealth increases, so often does cultural isolation. Loneliness and isolation feed anxiety, which leads to an attempt to accumulate more power and control. Reinhold Niebuhr wrote, "The will-to-power is thus an expression of insecurity even when it has achieved ends which, from the perspective of an ordinary mortal, would seem to guarantee complete security."

Letting go of the illusion of control is a terrifying and intimidating task. It takes courage and a belief in something greater than ourselves. For me, that faith is in God and the natural flow of nature and the universe. Revitalizing our spiritual connections will be discussed further in chapter 8.

SIMPLIFY AND PRIORITIZE

The more material possessions with which we burden ourselves, the more things we have to take care of in our lives. When I suddenly inherited my mother's fortune, I was filled with a terrible anxious need to control and organize it all perfectly. After several years of acquiring more and more "things" with my new-found wealth, I realized that my possessions were going to own me before too long. I had "bottomed out" emotionally with affluenza, and it soon became apparent that all my possessions had hastened, not cushioned my descent. Listening to the echoes from my childhood, I had told myself that a perfectly decorated mansion, with all the proper external paraphernalia, would ensure my emotional security and well-being. But just as my childhood home had failed to comfort me and make me feel safe, so did my re-creation of that illusion.

At that point I began a lifelong process of simplifying and prioritizing. During the last fifteen years, the way I spend money has changed dramatically. I tend to use it for services that simplify my life, making it easier and more manageable, leaving me with more time to spend with my children. I also like to travel, where the only things I accumulate are wonderful memories. I find that I am sharing my wealth with those around me with less fear that I might be taken advantage of. Recently, as my children have begun to turn into young women and pull away, I've begun to envision a future in which even more of my income will go to alleviate homelessness, hunger, and the abuse of women and children. I have faith that as the time draws near, my role in that process will become clearer.

REVERSING THE SLVER-SPOON SYNDROME: REPARENTING

Affluent families overly concerned with externals or outward form are fertile soil for narcissistic pathology, or the silver-spoon syndrome. In contrast to the narcissistic personality disorder, which is seen in individuals, the silver-spoon syndrome is a family phenomenon. Individual family members might exhibit this personality disorder, but more often with silver-spoon families free-floating narcissistic traits move and shift among the family members. Within the adults, and sometimes even in the children, this syndrome comes wrapped in the unappealing guise of the false grandiose self. This artificial "self" is rigid, defensive, possibly aggressive and paranoid, and highly protective.[15]

Interestingly, adults who were raised in narcissistic families are often not aware of having suffered any great emotional pain during their childhoods, despite ample evidence of genuinely traumatic experiences. I refer to this state of emptiness and lack of awareness as the "emotional void." This void leaves them detached and distant, and they have a difficult time connecting to their authentic feelings. It's almost as though their childhood traumas happened to someone else. Their memories are flat, one-dimensional, and hard to get a handle on.

Because of this emotional numbness, adults suffering from the silver-spoon syndrome seldom enter therapy. When they do, they present symptoms of chronic mild depression, emptiness, boredom, low self-awareness, lack of empathy, high pursuit of pleasure, lack of interest in work of any kind, and a belief that spending, travel, or other use of wealth will ease every frustration. Lives lacking in depth and content, combined with loneliness and despair underlie many of their problems. When a couple suffers from narcissistic pathology, they may not be able to tolerate true intimacy. Narcissists' defense mechanisms swing from one end of the pendulum to the other: from grandiosity, force, and tremendous self-importance to littleness, impotence, and raw vulnerability. It is sometimes difficult to see that people use this defense of "no other" unconsciously to protect themselves against further disappointment and hurt.

Much of my job as a therapist working with children, adults, or families suffering from affluenza and, more specifically, the silver-spoon syndrome, has been one of reparenting. In essence, I become, as in many client-therapist relationships, the parent they never had. Since many of their symptoms result from their inability to recognize, identify, or feel their feelings, I use the simple method of mirroring, which was discussed earlier in the book. As they begin to be able to discern what the different feelings and emotions are and how it feels to them individually to experience each one, they become more confident in their abilities to make mature, healthy decisions based on their hearts' response and their generally well-developed cognitive skills. In fact, many of these clients have over-developed cognitive abilities in compensation for their lack of feeling ability.

In addition to mirroring their feelings, I let them know that I have faith in their ability to move forward and meet the challenges that life presents. It is extremely rewarding to watch these children and adults as they begin to use their minds, hearts, and souls to identify, accept, and experience themselves as powerful, confident, and healthy people.

THE TWELVE STEPS

A Twelve Step meeting is a coming together of people who suffer from the same problem or addiction. These programs have arisen to meet almost every need and nearly every addictive/compulsive behavior. Twelve Step programs, founded on the principle of anonymity, provide a safe place for anyone, rich or poor, to seek support and encouragement in facing addiction. The common denominator of those who attend is the desire to stop a particular behavior, a goal that effectively cuts across all socioeconomic lines. Twelve Step programs exist in nearly every major city and in many smaller towns throughout the world. You can find a program near you by checking your local phone book. Twelve Step programs are free and provide an enormously valuable and easily accessible tool to use on the path of recovery.

I have only two criticisms of Twelve Step programs. In my experience, there is an underlying assumption that if you stop going to meetings, you will automatically relapse. I can speak from experience that this is not necessarily so. Knowing this prejudice, it was with great trepidation and hesitation that I took it upon myself to "graduate" from these programs and move on to other spiritual pursuits. I didn't relapse, my spirituality flourished, and I never regretted the decision to explore other avenues to spirituality and recovery. If you have been attending Twelve Step meetings for any substantial length of time and feel it is time to move on, I do think it is important to act to replace this support system with another type that better meets your spiritual needs. It is possible to outgrow a path we have traveled repeatedly. On the other hand, I have also returned to the Twelve Steps at various times and always received something of value from them.

My other criticism is of the covert hierarchy many Twelve Step programs create based on length of recovery. I believe there is an erroneous assumption that the duration of recovery is what counts most and that length of recovery automatically gives the "old-timers" the most authority and knowledge. This is not always the case. It is not the length of sobriety, or abstinence from the addictive substance or behavior, but the intensity of the experience and the breadth of learning and spiritual growth that determines the quality of one's recovery. In other words, it is the quality, not the quantity, that counts in the end.

USING THE PROGRAM

As part of her recovery, my client Jane has been attending Adult Children of Alcoholics (ACA) meetings. Because her mother committed suicide while active in AA, Jane has resisted a growing recognition that Twelve Step programs might be a useful tool for her own recovery. As her self-esteem and ability to process her feelings increase, however, she is overcoming her fear that she is just following in her mother's footsteps. What Jane is finding in our therapy sessions and her ACA meetings is her heart. A bright and intuitive woman, she only needed someone to help her access and validate her feelings. Although her new ACA friends might remind her of her mother's suicide, they have been emotionally available for her. She has been able to share some of her truth with them, and they have affirmed her and her feelings.

One of the issues Jane is working on with her ACA group and in her therapy is a new relationship with a very successful, powerful, and charismatic man who represents the "perfect," glittering life of the affluent. She has also been learning to express her emotions more easily and honestly, and to identify her problems. In sharp contrast to what she is learning in her therapeutic experiences, this man constantly encourages her to concentrate only on appearances and the external standards of success, which he believes are all that really count in life. As perfect and all-knowing as her lover seems, Jane is left feeling discounted and invisible, exactly as she did when she was a child. He is obviously, she has observed, her mother and father wrapped neatly into one package. Jane leaves the ACA meetings feeling good and grounded. She leaves Timothy feeling high in a frightening, out-of-control way, wondering whether she'll ever hear from him again and preparing herself for what she feels is his inevitable abandonment.

Although it is early in Jane's recovery process, her therapy and ACA meetings have helped her to realize that she is being presented with the perfect opportunity to reenact her childhood patterns. This time, however, she is an adult and has the tools and support to help her stay in touch with her own power and center. She has the chance to move through this experience to a higher and more complete understanding of who she really is and how she honestly feels about her life. If she can accomplish this, she can learn to make decisions based on her feelings, intuition, and knowledge—not based on the old tapes from her tragic childhood that are still playing in her head. With the help of her therapy and the solid support of the members of her ACA group, Jane has learned to identify the difference between her real needs and wants and the false values of affluenza. She is recovering her personal power at an amazing rate.

WOMEN AND ADDICTION

Although many people like Jane have been helped by the Twelve Step model of addiction intervention, this model is sometimes not as effective for women as it is for men. The first of the Twelve Steps begins, "We admitted we were powerless over . . ." In a culture where women have been socialized to be powerless, it does them no service to further emphasize their powerlessness over a substance that already has them on their knees. Men, on the other hand, are taught by society to fight and try harder. When one remembers that this particular model was developed by two powerful men, it stands to reason that this basic understanding of male-female socialization would be overlooked. It is also understandable given that the Twelve Step program was developed during a cultural period when masculine and feminine stereotypes were not closely examined. Fortunately, today there are a number of programs based on the Twelve Steps designed especially for women.

EMOTIONAL RELEASE EXERCISES

The story of Sara and Peter and the empty chair exercise in chapter 6 is a very good example of how emotional release work can aid in the treatment of affluenza. Although this type of work is more effectively and safely experienced in a therapeutic setting, a number of emotional release exercises can also be used by individuals on their own in an effort to facilitate the healing process—to connect and integrate one's "outsides" with one's "insides."

In intimate relationships, unexpressed rage and grief or displaced anger, inappropriately aimed at one's partner, are the main grist for the divorce mill. Feelings seldom wait for visits to the therapist's office to surface and demand attention. If each partner can learn to use certain tools to identify and release emotions appropriately, the relationship can stop being the battleground for past unresolved issues with other people or substances, such as money.

Effective tools for releasing feelings of rage include screaming your anger (hurt, sadness, shame, and so on) into a pillow in the privacy of your own room or another safe place. Some people feel awkward and foolish doing this and prefer the privacy of a closed car in an isolated parking lot. Others scream when they are driving along the freeway, where their yelling cannot be overheard. Another good way to discharge anger is to take an old bat, tennis racquet, or towel and beat the bed. If you are prone to violence, however, it is always better to choose a method of release that will not trigger further aggressive behavior. For instance, you might want to wring the towel rather than beat the bed with it. Throwing a good old-fashioned temper tantrum, kicking and screaming on the floor—again, in the privacy of your own room—is another good way to let off steam. Taking a long, energetic walk, stomping your feet, muttering, or yelling your discontent and anger out to God and the universe are other powerful ways to let go of pent-up emotions. If you are aware that affluenza is responsible for your repressed feelings, visualizing money and screaming your unhappiness about a specific incident concerning money are excellent ways to stay focused on the real root of your misery. By using emotional release work with affluenza, you will find that the emotional charge surrounding your beliefs around money will begin to diminish. In the future, actions or behaviors that are a result of those beliefs will be based on a less encumbered, more realistic, and healthier relationship with money.

JOURNALING AND LETTER WRITING

Journaling or letter writing is a sure and gentle path to the soul. The writing is just for you—the letters do not necessarily need to be sent, although they certainly may be. There is something profoundly healing about the flow of words from our hearts to the page that allows us to safely let go of feelings that are blocking our forward movement. Writing this book has been the single most healing exercise that I have undertaken. Although obviously not private, it is still written from the heart with honesty, much self-examination, and trepidation. Letting the feelings out has allowed me to proceed with my recovery and to take another step closer to God.

Following some basic guidelines can help make your journaling more productive. The first rule is to have no rules. Write as big and as sloppily as you like. Don't feel obligated to stay within the lines or write in complete sentences. Use different colors if you feel the urge. Stab the paper, rip it, wad it up, if you so desire. Throw it, burn it. Or keep it and cherish it. Perhaps it is a beautiful part of yourself that you have never been able to see clearly before. Maybe you will want to frame it, put it on the refrigerator, keep it forever. You may feel moved to intersperse your writing with pictures. Go for it. The sky's the limit. Remember it's all for you, an expression of your feelings, whatever they might be. Journaling is a wonderful way to spend time with that inner part of yourself. It's a nurturing, caring way to show how much you love yourself.

Writing a letter to express your feelings to someone is a particularly powerful tool for emotional release. It is always a good idea to wait a day or two after writing the letter before you decide whether you really want to send it or not. Often just the simple act of writing drains away the intensity of the feelings, and we realize that the other person doesn't need to receive the letter. We just needed to express the feelings and let go of the situation.

Early in my recovery, I went on a Fourth Step silent retreat as part of my AA Twelve Step program. Taking the Fourth Step involves making a list of all our defects (and assets) of character in preparation for turning them over to God in the next step. While doing this exercise, I came face to face with the immensity and power of my anger toward my father and his alcoholism. I realized that until I could begin to lay this anger to rest I was incapable of moving forward in my own recovery. Letting go of the rage became something that I needed to do for myself, not him, but at first it seemed impossible. I had carried it around with me for so long, it had become a major part of who I thought I was and of every relationship I had or didn't have. Along with my shame, it fueled all my addictions and compulsions.

One of the facilitators at the retreat suggested that I write my father a letter containing all of the things I had ever wanted to say to him. I wrote and cried for hours, going back many times over the next few days to reread it and, finally, to share it with someone I trusted. I never mailed the letter and, several years ago, I threw it away. It no longer resembled my feelings for my father.

About six months after writing the letter, I began to notice that the level of my anger had dropped. When I spoke to my father on the phone, what was said or not said no longer stayed with me for days after the call. I was better able to let go of the hurt. I began to see and *feel* that my father had done his best, that he loved me as much as he could. I also began to tell him, at the end of every phone conversation, that I loved him. It took him eight years to respond but, after that, we ended each and every conversation with those words. There is nothing more important, more healing, than getting back to the love in a relationship—any relationship. I thank God every day for showing me the way to forgive my father. It made my life whole.

Nondefensive and Nonoffensive Communication

Effective dialogue and confrontation requires a deep awareness of how we communicate defensively and offensively with others. Most of us are not aware how we have learned to communicate with our partners or of the patterns we have fallen into. To dismantle negative patterns we must relearn the very way we talk. Nondefensive responses are just that—we respond simply, without defending or attacking. The following is an example of a nondefensive response to an affluenza-related issue.

> Betty says, "All you ever think about is money! You never pay any attention to me or the kids."
> George responds, "What I hear you saying is that you feel hurt that I don't spend more time with you and the children. Maybe we could sit down and plan some family time together."

Although the tendency is to defend oneself in the face of such an attack and to retort in like manner, this disarming and nondefensive response reduces the emotional charge in the conversation and opens the line for honest communication. This is also an example of displaced anger; money is really not the issue.

Just as we can respond to confrontation nondefensively, we can also confront or communicate unpleasant feelings to others in a nonoffensive manner and receive better results. The key to this method is to stay focused on "I" statements: "I feel hurt. . . ," "I want. . . ," "I feel afraid. . . ," and so on. Be careful not to turn these statements around so that they become about the other person, i.e., "I feel that *you* . . ." Stay away from the past; try not to keep or bring up the score, "You did this then . . ." If you are trying to communicate nonoffensively, don't blame or criticize, threaten, or make any other inflammatory statements.

ACCESSING AND NURTURING THE INNER CHILD

In psychotherapeutic terms, the inner child is the little boy or girl within each of us, the shadow or reproduction of the little person we once were or perhaps weren't allowed to be as a child. It is the person we were before we were wounded. Unlike adults, children feel and express their feelings immediately and clearly, without shame. The socialization of society and families has not reached them yet with their gender-coded "shoulds" and "shouldn'ts."

As psychologists have begun to better understand the psychological importance of childhood experiences, they have begun to realize the healing, nurturing power of accessing and creating a partnership with that pretraumatized child within. There are few in the field of psychology today who do not use this powerful tool in some manner. Alice Miller and John Bradshaw are two well-known pioneers and proponents of inner-child work. My personal introduction to this model was at Onsite Training and Consulting, in Tucson, Arizona, through the work of Sharon Wegschieder-Cruse.

VISUALIZATION AND MEDITATION

"Checking in" with our inner child on a daily basis is a wonderful way to stay in touch with our true feelings. There are several ways to do this, and each gets easier and quicker with practice. One common method is to use a guided or creative visualization, preferably preceded by a relaxation exercise. Relaxing the body helps us to still the chatter of our minds and gives us greater access to our unconscious.

A guided visualization can be live or taped. Any good bookstore or library will carry audiotapes by a variety of people leading you through visualizations. Some people like to record their own voice reading the visualization; many of my clients have found this to be an additional aid in deepening their experience. Other people prefer the voice of their therapist. Another method is to do the visualization exercise with a friend who is willing to read the exercise out loud while you relax and enjoy it. It should be noted that creative visualization is used for a multitude of purposes, only one of which is to access the inner child.

Visualizing does not necessarily involve just seeing pictures on the inner screen of our minds. Any one of our senses—hearing, seeing, smelling, tasting, or touching—can be used in a visualization. For many people, sight is not the primary access sense. A musician, for example, might experience a visualization through patterns of sound. Other individuals might envision their inner child as rough and soft textures. Many people shy away from visualization because they think they just can't picture things mentally. But there is no right or wrong way to do this sort of meditation, and the only rule is to accept as valid whatever senses and impressions one experiences.[16]

The purpose of a guided visualization is to lead you gently through your mind's eye to a safe, quiet place created by the suggestions in the tape, reading, or talk. Many people use nature metaphors—wooded streams, open meadows, sunny beaches—to create a container in which they can imagine the form their specific feelings or problems will take. Once mentally in this place, the words of the visualization guide you gently through the mental process of releasing and letting go of those problems or symptoms. Many visualizations are aimed at specific goals such as anxiety reduction, weight loss, smoking cessation, grief reduction. In such instances, the metaphors and guidance in the visualization text will be more specific. You need only follow along.

This type of meditation is generally done sitting or lying down in a relaxed position with eyes closed. However, being relaxed doesn't mean you are helpless; you are always in total control during these exercises. If you begin to feel uncomfortable with what is happening, you can end the visualization by simply opening your eyes, turning off the tape, or leaving the room if you are in a group. At first, encountering unexpressed or repressed feelings might be difficult and emotionally painful. Quiet, deep, slow breathing and the knowledge that you can open your eyes will help you stay focused during these heightened emotional times. Unfortunately, it is often necessary to experience the pain before we can release it. If you are afraid that you will be overwhelmed by your feelings, ask for reassurance from your therapist or a friend. We have all been terrified by the enormity of our emotions at one time or another. It takes great courage to walk through many of our inner vistas that hold traumatic memories. Be patient, gentle, and kind with yourself. As time goes on, your visualizations will reflect your new level of emotional health and well-being, and the daily check-ins or more lengthy visualizations will become a great source of joy and strength. Your inner child, or inner self, is an instant and true barometer of your true feelings. Guided creative visualizations can leave you feeling grounded and connected to that which is real and important in your life.

Meditation is a powerful tool for healing our minds, bodies, and spirits. Along with guided visualizations, there are innumerable forms of meditation, used with countless goals in mind. Morning and evening are considered ideal times to meditate, with twenty minutes considered the minimum time by most proponents of meditation. Meditation is done with the eyes closed, in a relaxed position, normally either sitting or lying down, although there are "walking meditations" which obviously require open eyes and movement. You can be alone or in a large group. Meditation can be done with or without music and may or may not be guided by a live or taped voice. The goal of meditation is to quiet the busy clatter of the mind in order to allow contact with a spiritual source or center. Some people find a mantra useful in keeping them from daydreaming or other mental distractions. Others feel that we enter the meditative state by transcending our free-flowing thoughts through nonattachment to them or by becoming an objective observer of them. The actual act of meditating usually involves a quieting and slowing of the breathing process, in which our biological functions go into a resting mode and we are physically, as well as mentally, restored.

The type of meditation I prefer is self-guided and done to quiet, relaxing music. I unplug the phone or take it off the hook, put my two cats out (so they won't pick that particular time to leap onto my solar plexus for a brief nap!), lie down in a quiet room, and relax my entire body. I meditate for different reasons at different times, but often I go to meet my inner child in my "safe place," which I established in a guided meditation a number of years ago.

A safe place can be any place where you feel totally at ease, protected, warm, nurtured, and perhaps even energized. This could be a mountaintop, a meadow filled with flowers, a secret cottage, or an island in the middle of an ocean. Sometimes a safe place will spontaneously present itself to you, or you can create one by picking a setting that you love, mentally placing yourself in it, exploring it, experiencing its appearance, smells, textures, and sounds.

My safe place is a beach on a warm sunny day, with a gentle breeze blowing and the clear blue waves lapping gently at my feet. The sand is warm and I can feel the sun and breeze on my skin. When I go there, I am relaxed and open to receive whatever guidance is available for me. Most important, I am there to give myself a moment of quiet, reflective time, to listen to my heart, and to nurture myself.

Meditation is a very personal practice. The "right way" to meditate is the way that works best for you. For many years my perfectionism, my erroneous belief that there is a right way and a wrong way to do everything, got in the way of a few minutes of quiet reflection. So I would put my meditation off, believing that I needed to read a book or go to a class in order to do it correctly. In reality, all I really needed to do to find the peace I was looking for was to be quiet for a moment, find a quiet place, allow my thoughts to hush, and invite God, my higher power, my inner child, and whatever is good inside of me to guide me. It is the letting go of the need to control our lives, an acknowledgment that we are not the authors of this book, only the protagonist, that takes us out of the fear-driven race for some undefinable "there." Accepting that there is no "there" can hasten our letting go of the illusion that wealth is end-all and be-all.

As you become more familiar with creative visualization and meditation, you will find that they will become easier and easier. I can now simply relax, close my eyes, and instantly be in that safe place. What continues to amaze me is the speed with which I'm brought eye-to-eye with my true feelings. Staying in touch with my feelings centers me, focuses me, and clarifies my mission in life, at least for that day. It brings me closer to my spiritual source in a way that no other exercise does for me.

Psychodrama and Experiential Therapy

GRIEVING OUR LOSSES

When we do not mourn a deep loss fully, we condemn the unconscious to hold the magnitude of that pain and loss somewhere within itself. For the rest of our lives, each time we encounter an experience of intimacy that because of its depth of caring threatens to expose the wound to our conscious mind, we have to walk away. We walk away from ourselves, from the relationship, from our potential for love and life. We cannot go to that place of pain again, not because it hurt so much, but because we did not let it hurt enough. If we do not grieve, losing someone we love—whether through death, divorce or disease—becomes a loss of ourselves.[17]

In our culture today, particularly among the affluent, sadness and grief are not encouraged, sometimes not even acceptable. After all, what do the rich have to be sad about? All that money is supposed to make us happy. Looking good, happy, and successful, is promoted and prized. Women are taught from an early age to put a smile on their faces and keep "a stiff upper lip." Men, particularly of the current middle and older generations, continue to struggle with self-destructive messages from within and without that disavow and disallow the expression of their feelings.

Since we live in the age of Prozac and Zoloft, what money can't do the "happy" pills will. Antidepressants serve a serious and worthwhile cause when used in conjunction with therapy for the chronically depressed. They are not meant to be another quick fix or another substance to distract us from that all-important task of grieving both the small and major losses in our everyday lives. When did we start to think that there was something wrong with sadness? Tears are the gateway to the soul. It is tragic to think that we continue to discourage and disparage the healing process that would bring us home—to ourselves, to our relationships, to "our potential for love and life."

Recently, at my daughter's school, I attended a talk given by Mary Pipher, author of *Reviving Ophelia: Saving the Selves of Adolescent Girls.* One of the main ideas Pipher tries to communicate to her young clients is the truth that it is easier to feel the pain now than to face the results later of self-medicating, addictive behaviors—drinking, drugs, sex, eating disorders—that might, for the moment, allow them to escape the distress in their lives. What teenagers and anyone who self-medicates doesn't realize is that, along with extending the suffering, they are killing themselves. Each time they choose a numbing alternative over an authentic feeling, no matter how painful that feeling may be, they have failed to mourn, failed to grieve. They have taken another step away from the ability to know themselves or anyone else, a step away from the ability to be whole. When we avoid the pain of loss through means of medication or addictive substances or behaviors, we are, ironically, prohibiting our ability to feel emotions at the other end of the pendulum—joy and happiness. We plod on, leading lives of quiet desperation.

REGAINING OUR JOY

Psychodrama and experiential therapy are two very powerful spiritual tools for accessing both our repressed grief and our lost joy. By creating a safe therapeutic structure for individuals to experience their feelings, past and present, these forms of therapy help the grieving process to move forward, creating space for intimacy to become possible. "Psychodrama can be defined, therefore, as the science which explores the 'truth' by dramatic methods."[18] Psychodrama is the mother of experiential therapy and a more extensive method for deep healing. The technique uses six main instruments: (1) the stage; (2) the subject, patient, or protagonist (the person whose story is being enacted); (3) the double (the inner voice of the protagonist); (4) the director (the person or therapist directing the psychodrama); (5) the staff of therapeutic aids, auxiliary egos or group members playing the other parts in the psychodrama; and (6) the audience or other group members.

Role-playing is an integral part of both psychodrama and experiential therapy. Both methods allow a repressed memory or problem to surface onto the present "stage" or group setting and to be reenacted and released in a safe, nurturing setting. People are like computers with feelings—we store everything that happens to us, both good and bad, somewhere in our memories. There are layers of memories, some easy to retrieve and others more inaccessible. Early childhood traumas that were suppressed because they threatened the sanity of a young child can be retrieved, felt, and released through psychodrama. What our fragile psyches could not bear as children or younger adults can be safely integrated into our mature personalities with the care and guidance of a skilled therapist. By releasing our trauma, we are clearing a space to begin to receive the joy, serenity, and happiness available to us in the present. I have had the good fortune to do a lot of my personal recovery work and my professional training at Onsite Training and Consulting in Tucson, Arizona. Many locations throughout the country, however, offer psychodrama and experiential therapy.

Both traditional therapy and psychodrama advocate the release of pent-up emotions. Whereas traditional therapy is more focused on exploring these feelings by talking about them in the past tense, psychodrama is designed to express them in the here and now through action. In my professional and personal experience, there is simply no comparison between the two. Psychodrama and experiential therapy can accomplish in hours what it might take traditional therapy years to access and process.

If you wish to explore psychodrama, I recommend an initial inpatient experience followed by a commitment to participate in a weekly experiential or psychodramatic therapy group in your area. See the resource section for additional information.

During a recent psychodrama experience in which I was involved, a woman named Jan was able to experience her need as a young child for strength to survive in a home steeped in sadness and misery. It became clear that her feelings of isolation and irrelevance in her parents' lives were the source of her need to turn to a drink, a man, or food to feel comfort and safety. She used those things to shore up her courage to demand the attention and love that she so desperately needed to grow and survive. As she saw for the first time the reasons behind her addictions, it became easier to forgive herself for her mistakes.

Psychodrama frequently provides us with a powerful physical release, a visceral reaction to the work that signals a huge, healing step forward. In the exercise described above, Jan reported that she could actually feel the shame of her abusive relationship with food rising to the surface of her skin, where she literally wiped it away. The result of this experience is that Jan has become consistently tuned into whether she is eating because of physical hunger or simply trying to satisfy an unmet psychological need. She has lost her unhealthy emotional connection to food along with fifty-four pounds without any apparent effort. Now able to set emotionally appropriate boundaries in her relationships, she has been able to "let go" of the false protection of her excess weight.

It is difficult to change, even for those of us with the best of intentions and determination. Our ego, driven by our fears, will try to find many ways to distract us from our chosen path of recovery. It knows that these tools and this time brings healing and growth of the true Self, a process that diminishes our controlling, self-serving false ego. Fear drives us away from ourselves. The longer we run and the farther we travel, the more difficult it becomes and the stronger the "travel aids" must be.

For many of us who are accustomed to the quick fixes that wealth can afford, the slower, more subtle tools of therapy or spirituality are difficult to adopt. Not only must we face our inner turmoil in order to quiet it with meditative practices, but doing so will take some time, discipline, and practice. Sooner or later we will surely be faced with whatever we fear the most. If we have the determination and faith to continue, we will without a doubt find healing. It just may not come as quickly as we would like it to. It is often difficult to take time away from the chaos of our lives, but even spending a few minutes a day connected with our inner selves will cause us to reap enormous psychological benefits. In our culture, we are socialized to search for answers outside of ourselves. When we shift our focus within, the results are truly astonishing. We may find what we really fear the most is the realization that we *can* be all that God meant us to be. There are no longer any excuses.

NOTES

1. A. Toufexis, "The Woes of Being Wealthy," *Time,* 29 February 1988, 95.

2. Marc Miringoff and Marque-Luisa Miringoff, "America's Social Health: The Nation's Need to Know (Special Report: Social Indicators)," *Challenge* 38, no. 5 (1995): 19.

3. Betsy Morris, "Big Spenders: As a Favored Pastime, Shopping Ranks High with Most Americans," *Wall Street Journal,* 30 July 1987.

4. Laurence Shames, *The Hunger for More: Searching for Value in an Age of Greed* (New York: W.W. Norton & Co., 1994), 147.

5. "Trust Fund: Blessing . . .", interview with John Levy, *More Than Money,* no. 9 (Autumn 1995), 6.

6. Anne Slepian and Christopher Mogil, "Twelve Ways to Keep Trust Funds from Messing Up Your Kids," *More Than Money,* no. 9, (Autumn, 1995) 8–9.

7. Joyce LeBeau, "The 'Silver-Spoon Syndrome' in the Super Rich: The Pathological Link of Affluence and Narcissism in Family Systems," *American Journal of Psychotherapy* 42 (1988): 428.

8. Daniel Goleman, *Emotional Intelligence* (New York: Bantam Books, 1995), 81, 82.

9. Ibid., 81-83.

10. James Hillman, "A Contribution to Soul and Money" (Soul and Money: Proceedings of the 8th International Congress of the International Association for Analytical Psychology held in August 1980 in San Francisco), Spring Publication, 42.

11. Henry C. Lindgren, *Great Expectations: The Psychology of Money* (Los Altos, Calif.: William Kaufmann, Inc., 1980), 77.

12. Louis Gould, "Ticket to Trouble," *New York Times Magazine,* 23 April 1995, 41.

13. Ibid., 40.

14. Ibid., 40.

15. LeBeau, "The 'Silver-Spoon Syndrome' in the Super Rich," 425–28.

16. For further information about visualization, refer to Anna Wise *The High Performance Mind* (Tarcher/Putnam, 1996).

17. Tian Dayton, *The Quiet Voice of Soul: How to Find Meaning in Ordinary Life* (Deerfield Beach, Fla.: Life Health Communications, 1995), 128.

18. J. L. Moreno, *Psychodrama and Group Psychotherapy* (McLean, Va.: Beacon House, 1972), A.

8

THROUGH THE EYE
OF A NEEDLE

Then said Jesus unto his disciples, "Verily I say unto you that a rich man shall with difficulty enter into the kingdom of heaven.

And again I say unto you, it is easier for a camel to go through the eye of a needle than for a rich man to enter into the kingdom of God."

MATTHEW 19:23–24

I am thankful to have the money to do the work I am called to do: transforming money into the currency of spirit.

From a letter to *More Than Money*

In the past, the emotional prognosis for the wealthy has not been good. As we have seen, inherited fortune can be—as Leonie Walker, 1989 Director of the Women Managing Wealth program in New York City, calls it—a "cruel karmic joke."[1] The wealthy, who appear to have everything—or could if they so desired—are often missing the most important things in life: an identity, a role, a job, an intimate connection with others. They are so camouflaged by their wealth, that it is difficult for them or anyone else to see the reality of the person beneath the disguise.

Rich or poor, it is a challenge to all human beings to create a satisfying and worthwhile life. In that sense, we are all alike. The difference in the challenge for the rich is finding a healthy, balanced life *in spite of* their affluence. We have demonstrated throughout this book how, when playing the game of life with all its inherent ups and downs is voluntary, when much of the risk is eliminated, one loses a great deal of life's richness and complexity. A sense of emptiness develops, a lingering despondency which stems from a feeling that something has been left unfinished.

One quickly understands, however, that few in our culture will be disposed to give recognition or sympathy for such a condition. "I should be so unfortunate" is a common response. "That's one problem I'd be glad to have!" For the very poor, as well as for those who feel trapped in unfulfilling, dead-end jobs, or who don't know if they'll even have a job tomorrow or enough to retire or enough to provide for their children's educations, the belief that a windfall would solve all their problems is understandable. As Philip Slater points out in his book *Wealth Addiction*, "Money can . . . provide genuine relief of pain. For poor people, this is one of the primary meanings money has."[2] Given this fact, it is not hard to see how wealthism develops. In a very real sense, the non-wealthy are as vested in the delusion that rich means happy as the wealthy are. If one assumes, as most in our culture do, that money equals fulfillment and power and freedom from stress, fear, or doubt, then what's the problem? What will it take to satisfy the rich, anyway? The real question is, however, if money doesn't bring happiness, then what will it take to satisfy *us*, those without big bankbooks. If not money, or the dream of it, then what?

I, too, have been guilty of wealthism—prejudice against my own economic class. This prejudice is, in many ways, another form of denial. I have often avoided the company of the rich and sought the company of people of average wealth in an attempt to somehow prove that I was not like *them*, not like the rich. *I* wasn't a snob; *I* wasn't insensitive to the plight of the common person. *I* preferred relationships with men of average means, assuming that those at my own economic level would be shallow and callous. I have assumed the worst of a group of people with whom I now find myself doing therapeutic work. I am sorry to say I have treated others the way that I most fear being treated.

Wealthism is one of the most painful, lonely, and alienating aspects of affluence. It sets the rich apart from their fellow human beings at a time in their lives when they are supposedly the most "successful." It is confusing and bewildering for the newly rich when relationships go unexpectedly askew. Hoping to bask in the glory of their newly acquired wealth (a terribly naive and, perhaps, irresponsible fantasy), they may find "groupies" all too eager to befriend them, and old friends who have become uncomfortable and ill at ease.

People who are born into wealth often have a different response to wealthism than the recent rich. For some, perhaps, it has lost its "sting" because they have always been exposed to it. They may even believe, due to feelings of shame, that they deserve to be treated in a derogatory manner, and therefore do little to change the circumstances. For most people who grow up with wealth, however, the awareness of the resentment and antipathy of others may be felt but only vaguely comprehended. The invisible walls of the golden ghetto which set them apart in the world may diffuse those prejudices and make them impossible to fathom. That cultural insularity may also provide a multitude of rationalizations with which the wealthy try to explain it all away: "they" are just ill-bred people, "they" want what's not rightfully theirs, "they" are merely envious. (For the nonwealthy who also suffer from affluenza, of course, the latter is almost certainly true.)

Yet either way, the segregation of classes is enormously damaging to all involved, affluent or not, and to society as a whole. Our environment is degraded by the unexamined pursuit of profits; more and more of our children are ill-fed, ill-educated, and abused as the poor become poorer and greater in number; and our infrastructure continues to crumble as resources never seem to end up where they are most needed. So what is it that needs to be done?

As American society is losing its middle class, as the disparity between rich and poor widens, and as violence, hatred, and crime increase proportionately to the economic injustices, we are seeing a return to fortressed communities and homes with bars on the windows and weapons under the beds. This fear and the violence that incites it are a logical and painful extension of the unresolved racial and class issues in this "land of opportunity." But as fear and mistrust increase among the wealthy and between economic classes, the available affluence in our world ceases to circulate and that chasm between the "haves" and the "have nots" just grows and grows. The result is that we as a world become poorer, in every sense of the word.

Although humanity has literally been given the resources of the entire world, we have continued to take and take with little, if any, thought of what an existence devoid of giving actually produces. We are entering a crucial time in our history, and the warning signs are clear. The "me" generation of the seventies and eighties was a result of our accumulated cultural "dis-ease" with money, and a lack of financial and spiritual generosity. America has 5 percent of the world's population and uses 25 percent of its resources, and 1 percent of the people in this country control 45 percent of the available wealth—approximately the same amount as controlled by the bottom 90 percent.[3] If we continue to selfishly hoard our material and spiritual wealth, civilization will surely self-destruct.

With great urgency, we need to find ways to build bridges across class barriers. We need to re-envision ourselves as a community rather than isolated economic islands in a vast, shark-infested cultural sea. This new vision will certainly involve redistributing wealth to some degree, but until we correct our cultural delusions about what money is and how we should relate to it, redistributing money is simply passing around our fears, hatreds and dysfunctions. Changing one ideology's economic system for that of another is futile. Both Marxism and capitalism are based, after all, on the erroneous assumption that the soul of mankind is economic. As long as we continue to believe that, system changes are merely repeated episodes of "meet the new boss, same as the old boss."

The paradigm must begin to shift from one in which we use others as stepping stones to the top, pushing them further down in our materialistic frenzy, to one where we grow and expand together, each person an essential part of the abundance shared by all.

What I am describing is nothing less than a spiritual awakening. In addiction recovery terms, a spiritual awakening is the acceptance of a power greater than oneself which, when humbly sought, can heal the addictive/compulsive drive that made our lives unmanageable. Accepting the primacy of a spiritual reality, admitting our powerlessness over the mess we've made of our lives and our world, and turning our will and lives over to some unseen power is the most difficult task in recovery from dysfunctional behaviors. One can imagine how much more difficult it will be for the affluent who are waist deep in the material world; conditioned to see themselves almost exclusively in terms of financial assets and social status; fearful and suspicious of the motives of others; and hated, envied, or both, by the majority in our culture.

I contend that the solution to our misery, mistrust, destructive behaviors, and emotional dysfunctions is beyond economic and political reform, and even, ultimately, beyond psychotherapy. The answers for the next millennium will come from within, from a greater individual and collective awareness of our spiritual nature.

My Journey to Alcoholics Anonymous

Looking for a spiritual answer often first occurs to us when we "bottom out" from the devastation of addiction. Some time before I began to understand the pernicious effects of affluenza in my life, I reached bottom as a result of alcoholism.

My emotional and spiritual bankruptcy became clear to me shortly after the birth of my first daughter, Rebecca. I remember the exact moment when I began to question my dependence upon alcohol. It was a Saturday morning as I stood by the bar in our kitchen mixing my standard Bloody Mary in preparation to go outside and push my daughter on the swing. Impatient with waiting she finally asked, "Mommy, why do you need a drink?" This question stopped me dead in my tracks as the truth of what I had become began to slowly seep through the denial. In that moment, I glimpsed a light at the end of the tunnel, and it was indeed, as they say, a train.

Until that morning, buried beneath the guise of my addiction to sugar and food, alcohol had simply been more calories to count. The pain of hangovers, the fear of blackouts, the intense shame unleashed by my daughter's question, the unhappiness in my marriage—all of these brought me stumbling finally to my knees in the knowledge that perhaps I did not have everything in my life figured out. In fact, I was a mess. Unmanageable did not begin to describe it. I began slowly to turn and face my alcoholism.

My spiritual awakening began with Alcoholics Anonymous sixteen years ago. I have never forgotten the miracle that took place the first time I walked into an AA meeting. By the grace of God—for I know that no human power could have done it—my desire to drink was lifted and I came "home" again. My soul relaxed in the comfort of that fellowship and I felt an immediate sense of recognition and security. I knew in a way that I had never experienced before that I was, perhaps for the first time, right where I needed to be.

Through my own experiences and my work with my clients I have come to believe that addicts are a chosen people. It doesn't matter what the addiction is about: drugs, alcohol, food, sex, gambling, money. What matters is the bottoming out and, finally, the climb back up. When we begin to turn our lives around, the substance or behavior that nearly destroyed us is transformed into the doorway to our salvation.

Most people go through life never really having to face themselves, their deepest problems and fears. The only road to recovery from addictions is to confront the demons head-on and to transform and overcome them. Ironically, we "overcome" by surrendering our will to God, as we understand Him/Her, and admitting our powerlessness over the addictive substance or behavior. It is a difficult and challenging process in a society where willpower is held in such high esteem. But surrender is the first step toward freedom from our addictions and compulsions. It is also the beginning of the road to recovery from affluenza and all its destructive implications.

Only you and your higher power know the way for you. I can only tell you where I've been and what worked for me. Other people recovering from affluenza can walk a part of the path with you and by so doing, help you along the way. But beware of those who tell you that their way is the only way. If they are in a place of needing to push or pull you along, you can be pretty sure they haven't found enlightenment yet. Enlightenment is an overused and misunderstood word anyway. For me, it simply means that the spiritual path can be for the most part a lighted one, that we no longer are left to stumble aimlessly and alone in the dark. In any event, I guarantee that you are the only one who knows where your light switch is! So watch out for the high-pressure salesman, the guy who offers you a deal, but only if you sign up now. The true spiritual path, whichever one it might be for you, will be one of attraction, not recruitment.

What Is Spirituality?

Spirituality is our own unique connection to God, or the "spirit" of God, however we might define that for ourselves. It is an internal message, a "still, small voice" that guides and comforts us. Whether we call this inner communication the voice of God, a higher power, a deeper consciousness, or intuition, it is up to us to decide. There are as many spiritual paths as there are people, and each of us must find our own way. In a material world that appears to be governed by scarcity and danger, finding one's way in invisible realms can seem a daunting task. Yet at other times, it is as though God has given us a road map and lit our way in neon signs, and that we only need lift a foot and the knowledge of where to set it down is ours. Spirituality is a reminder that there are, indeed, miracles in the world and, mysteriously and gratefully, we are a part of them.

As we recognize our mortality, most of us begin to yearn for the spiritual. We begin to feel the lack of something in our lives, an absence. The gaping hole that has always seemed to have been a part of our beings yawns a little wider and urges us to find a way to fill it. Often by this time in our lives we've begun to realize that many of the old standbys—the usual comforts, such as the material things, addictions, even loved ones—don't quite fill the void. Neither fat investment portfolios nor the ego gratification of worldly success seem to work, either. There is something beyond all this, not of this world or of our physical senses, that we must somehow bring into intimate relationship with our deepest selves, our souls. The difficulty and challenge, and ultimately the success of living a life in which spirituality plays a vital role, comes from finding the spiritual practice that suits each of us individually. Walking the path of the spiritual is intensely personal and, alternately, the most difficult and the most simple of tasks. The sacred and the spiritual are forever intertwined and nurture our ability to be intimate and available in our relationships. It speaks to us through the voices of people in our lives—even when we don't listen and don't like what we hear.

A connection with the spiritual comes to us through the lessons in our lives, often through our struggles and pain. As human nature would have it, we turn to God most fervently when we are in great need and often forget to nurture the connection when all is well. Author and lecturer Marianne Williamson talks about how easy it was for her to go along in life paying no attention to God until something went wrong, at which point she would fall to her knees and pray for help. After she received the help and life had righted itself, time and again she would return to her old ways. It occurred to her after a while that perhaps her life would go better all the time if she just stayed on her knees.[4]

My spirituality has come to me through gifts from God, gently over the years. It comes when I am writing, through my desire to communicate and to connect with others. It is present in my painting—again, born of a passion for something of beauty that I am striving to reproduce. It binds and deepens my relationships with people I love. It gives meaning to an otherwise meaningless life. It has opened me to a world of wonder and bright, new possibilities.

God is always present in our lives, waiting patiently for us to turn and ask for help. Asking for guidance, turning our lives and relationships over to a higher power, praying for the willingness and the courage to let go, letting go in the face of my fear, and at the end of the day, being grateful for another day lived in God's presence are the cornerstones of any spiritual practice.

After my father died, the loneliness and pain I felt seemed overwhelming, at times, terrifying. In the midst of my grief, I turned again to my spiritual practices. I read books about grieving and loss, called healthy friends, and listened through my tears to their assurances that time would heal this pain, that the grief would not overwhelm me, that I would be strong again. I prayed, meditated, saw my therapist, wept, read, exercised, ate healthy, nourishing food, went to Twelve Step meetings, and answered the many expressions of sympathy from my friends and family with gratitude and love.

Crying to a friend on the phone, I said, "It hasn't worked!" When he asked me what I wanted, I said, "To feel better." He started laughing and said gently, "Jessie, you know the only way through the pain is to feel it."

The hardest thing to remember, and sometimes the most difficult to live with, is that our lessons in life are taught on God's timetable, not ours. The rainbow at the end of the storm is surely there, it is just not up to us when the storm will be over. We pray for the willingness to hold on, the willingness to believe that in fact, there is a rainbow. Sometimes it is impossible for us to feel God's presence in our lives because of the loneliness and sorrow. Then my definition of spirituality becomes the faith to simply keep hoping and believing in the face of the darkness and anguish.

Many people are comfortable finding their spirituality within traditional religions and there are churches to fit nearly every belief system. The structure and security of the liturgy, rituals, and the sense of family that comes from being part of a religious community add greatly to the appeal of these institutions. Meeting on a regular basis to worship God supports many people in their spiritual practices and reminds them to continue on their own.

Others have become disillusioned with more traditional or orthodox theologies or have been deeply wounded and oppressed by them. These individuals may find their spirituality outside of a formal religious practice. Some traditional religious structures seem to perpetuate, condone, and even celebrate the materialism and madness of the American dream. This message is even more insidious when delivered under the guise of religion. But ultimately, it is not important where you find your worship or what particular form it takes, only that you make a place for the spiritual in your life.

Finding the sacred in everyday life is an essential part of defining your own spirituality. The sacred comprises those people, places, and things that connect you to the greater whole. Their very presence in your life calls you to a greater and deeper spirituality, an ever-growing connection to your higher power. For example, down the street from a house we had in Florida, there is a park with a perfect ring of hundred-year-old Banyan trees, tall, shaded with branches intertwined and roots reaching deep into the earth. In their presence, I am immediately brought back to my connection to God, so surely do I feel that this spot is a sacred place.

Living consciously in search of the sacred, striving to listen to our hearts, nurturing our souls, watching our lives unfold with faith that there is a greater plan, that every moment is a gift from God given to us with infinite love for the purpose of our higher learning and good—these practices will lead us unfailingly to a clear sense of mission and meaning in our lives.

Openness and Trust

Teilhard de Chardin wrote, "Instead of standing on the shore and proving to ourselves that the ocean cannot carry us, let us venture on its water just to see." The older (and, I hope, wiser) I get, the more certain I am that there are no mistakes. As I look back on my life, I see a pattern leading me with patience and persistence to where I am now. Unfortunately, it is rarely easy to see that pattern when we are in the midst of it. Often the next step is not so clear until after we have taken it. At these times more than any other, we need to trust in a universal intelligence that is greater than our own.

I have a client, Tally, who has used a unique variation of the geographical cure in her therapy. (The "geographical cure," a term coined in Alcoholics Anonymous, refers to the desire to escape one's inner turmoil by relocating physically—"If only I could get to California, *then* I could get my life together.") Whenever we would be about to move forward and confront another problem, she would begin talking about moving. She would spend weeks considering the possibility that perhaps all she needed was a change of scenery and a new place to live to solve her problems. Interestingly, it wasn't really a new place, but a particularly posh resort town where she had been sent to live as a young woman shortly after having a nervous breakdown. It held an allure for her that no amount of talking seemed to change. However, when she would actually consider going, she would become terrified and move on to some other defense to stall the inevitable progress that she continued to make in therapy. Eventually the cycle would be complete and she would be left once again facing herself and able to finally move forward.

Recently, as fate would have it, Tally was offered an opportunity to house-sit in that resort town. After some deliberation, she bravely decided to take the offer and began to face all her fears and anxieties associated with returning. She trusted that this was the next "right" thing for her to do, and indeed it was. She has increased her therapy to twice a week and is using this opportunity to grow in leaps and bounds. She is beginning to touch on the deep anger, a legacy from a childhood of abandonment and abuse. As she expresses the anger and releases it, the depression that has led her on several occasions to consider suicide begins to lessen, her sense of control over her life increases, her self-esteem grows, and her faith in a higher power and process is nurtured.

Tally has always been very uncomfortable with the concept of God; many people are. For some it may be easier to avoid the word, to think in terms of a power greater than oneself (as in Twelve Step meetings), a universal intelligence, or simply intuition. It's even okay to refer to it, as Woody Allen once did, as that "great Maybe in the sky." It's a start, anyway! Regardless of the name we give it, tuning in to that inner voice involves a process of slowing down and adopting a listening posture of openness and humility. We pray in acknowledgment that we don't know what to do—not some of the time, but most of the time or even all of the time. Getting to that place of letting go can be terrifying.

Trust in an invisible higher power is difficult, particularly since we have so often trusted in people who may have, at the very least, let us down, and at the worst, damaged us emotionally or physically. It often seems easier and saner to simply live with the illusion that *we* are in control, until once again we run smack into another brick wall. If we listen carefully in the silence that follows the fall, we will hear a voice gently lifting and guiding us to a new and better place. But we have to listen. It sounds so simple and yet few people seem able to do this. I shake my head in wonder as I write this, thinking of how often I have to relearn the very lesson I'm trying to express here. Then I remember: We teach what we need to learn.

Prayer and Faith

A friend suggested to me recently that an atheists' worst moment may be when he or she is feeling grateful and there is no one to thank. When I began my recovery from alcoholism, I was an atheist most of the time and a pantheist some of the time, so my religious beliefs ranged from none to believing that God existed within the forms of nature. Since I found it difficult to believe in God at all, and even harder to pray, I fell back on the advice of AA old-timers. Two suggestions were particularly helpful, starting me on the road to a rich, deeply satisfying relationship with the God of my understanding. The first was that I begin by "praying for the willingness to be willing" to believe and pray. The second was for me to "act as if" I believed in a higher power, and to pray as if I believed. I don't know exactly how long I relied on those two "tricks," but before long I was willing to pray, and believing was no longer an act. My favorite prayer is the Serenity Prayer, a cornerstone of the Twelve Step programs:

God, grant me the serenity
To accept the things I cannot change,
The courage to change the things I can,
And the wisdom to know the difference.

A shorter version, one that is helpful for beginners, is

I can't.
God can.
I think I'll let God.

The wonderful thing about prayer is that it can be done anytime, anywhere. Many people feel more comfortable taking an informal approach to prayer, simply carrying on a conversation with God—sharing a running commentary on their lives. Others go to elaborate shrines or create an "altar" within their homes, praying on bended knee, or prostrating themselves in front of an image or symbol of their God. In all major religions, days are set aside for prayer, and all spiritually oriented people experience times when they spend more time praying, times when they feel the need of more guidance and comfort.

I believe that our prayers are always answered. The answers may not be the ones we want, but they are always the ones we need. There is a wonderful saying, "Be careful what you pray for, you may get it." Sometimes the path to the answer is a long and difficult one. For instance, to find the one true, lasting, loving relationship in our lives, we may have to go through a lot of "learning" relationships. We may not see today that God is in fact answering our prayer in His/Her own time and that our part is to learn our lessons along the way so that we are ready for the relationship when it comes along. If we are busy doing things our way, trying to make princes or princesses out of toads, we may very well miss the "right" relationship when it taps us on the shoulder. Our confusion and frustration stems from our impatience and our fear. To assuage these feelings, we want to have everything, all the answers, right *now*. Trust and faith in our higher power, believing that what is meant to be will be, are two essential and powerful tools on the spiritual journey.

Faith is believing that the prayers will work, an important part of letting go of the need to control the outcome of events ourselves. Having faith is where many of us get tripped up. Marianne Williamson, author of *A Return to Love,* says, "Faithlessness is not lack of faith but faith in nothing. . . . Faith is an aspect of consciousness. We either have faith in fear or we have faith in love, faith in the power of the world or faith in the power of God."[5]

Facing Our Fear

What brings many of my clients to their spiritual path is, in some ways, a simple process of elimination. They begin to see that doing things their way, attempting to control every situation in their lives, has not brought them any closer to the serenity and fullness that they yearn for. When all else fails, they finally become willing to try it a different way. Letting go and "acting as if" there is a greater plan beyond their own has brought them moments of joy, and an ability to fully savor the present in all its wonder. The realization that they don't have to do it all can also bring a huge sense of relief. Human beings always experience a certain amount of fear when they begin to do things differently. We are creatures of habit, and no matter how uncomfortable our old ways may have been, they are familiar. A new path, even a better one, is scary.

Amazingly and through the grace of God, when we begin to turn and face that fear within us, we are given the strength and hope not only to survive in the face of it, but to flourish and grow in ways that we had never found possible before. For there is no resistance when we begin to walk in synch with the universe, with God, with whatever we choose to call that power that is within us and yet not of us.

The delayed gratification of the inner spiritual path is not the instant fix that we are so used to in our externally focused culture. The rewards, however, are greater and the effects longer-lasting. Our growing sense of well-being and self-worth are strong incentives for us to continue once we have begun. It becomes easier and easier to have faith in a higher power, God, the universe, or simply in our inner selves, as we begin to see and feel the astonishing results.

When I am working with my clients I encourage them not only to look within for the right questions (psychotherapy), but to keep looking within for the eventual answers (spiritual listening). With loving support from people who care about us, we can learn to relax and trust that part of us which is there for our higher good. As I support my clients in their psychotherapeutic journey, they begin to identify their real feelings, some of them for the first time since they were children. As adults, then, they learn that they can face the terror that so overwhelmed them in childhood. They begin to understand which behaviors in their lives represent running from childhood fears and that with time, they can learn to put those self-defeating, shame-based behaviors aside and choose ones that nurture and expand their true selves. As I support them to look inside spiritually, they begin to understand that their true self is connected to others, to the world around them, and to God, and that the guidance they need for living day to day is available to them just for the asking.

Are Spirituality and Wealth Incompatible?: Simplifying and Letting Go

Wealth and the pursuit of the spiritual life have seldom been seen as compatible. There is a long-standing belief in many theologies that the authentic religious life, one dedicated to the service of God, is best attained through a state of poverty. Some religious orders require vows of poverty. There are religions whose laity live in abject poverty while the priesthood lives in opulent splendor. I believe the quicksilver nature of money often *does* make wealth an impediment to the quiet, contemplative state that is part of the spiritual quest. Money easily and often translates into material possessions, and quite simply, possessions take time to acquire, time to maintain, and even time to dispose of. There is a reason why one cannot serve two masters at the same time.

The allure of the ticker-tape might easily outweigh the quiet calling of a beautiful sunset or a peaceful moment spent in prayer. It is not surprising that the glitter of gold captures many an eye when coupled with the misconception that believing in God is all we have to do. Belief is just the starting point. The spiritual life requires nurturing and discipline if it is to flourish. It requires full attention. It requires *time.*

In Buddhism, non-attachment to the material world is a prerequisite for spiritual advancement. In the New Testament passage that concludes with the difficulties of a rich person getting into heaven, Jesus tells a young man to sell all his possessions, give the money to the poor and come follow him, "if you wish to go the whole way." The young man had observed that he followed the commandments but still felt that he somehow fell short. In the end, the young man went away with a heavy heart because "he was a man of great wealth." It is then that Jesus observes that it's easier to get a camel through the eye of a needle than a rich man into heaven. In Aramaic, the original language of the Gospels, the word for "camel" and the word for "rope," *gamla,* are homonyms. Thus, one could argue that the correct translation of the passage would be, "It is easier for a rope to go through the eye of a needle than for a rich man to enter into the kingdom of God."[6] (Besides lending metaphorical sense to the passage, this translation improves the odds for the rich considerably.)

The point is that Jesus is never reported to have said that possessing wealth disqualified one for salvation. If one held on to that wealth rather than take the opportunity for spiritual growth, however, it would become a definite impediment. Money, remember, is *not* the root of all evil: it is the *love* of money that causes problems.

Though it is perhaps more difficult to live a simple life when one is wealthy, it is certainly possible. Succeeding at the art of living is a matter of focus and intent. Remembering the absolute transformational quality of money, we can begin to go beyond mere acquisition to the creation of abundance in each life we touch. There is great spiritual truth in the saying "What goes around, comes around." As you give to others, materially and spiritually, it will come back multiplied to you.

In many ways this type of giving is an extension of letting go and trusting. We are letting go of many of the material manifestations of wealth, if not the money itself, and trusting that what comes to fill that void will be of greater spiritual value than what we had before. We strive to have faith that the spiritual satisfaction will outweigh the material satisfaction. We use the spiritual tools that we have discovered to release the fear that would stop us from letting go of a life of materialism and affluenza.

After we shift our focus from the external world to the internal, there is a period of time when the newness and uncertainty of our path may appear downright unappealing. Change is always difficult but this one in particular can pose innumerable obstacles along the way. Shifting from the concrete and visible to the invisible realm of the spirit is no easy feat. For the wealthy, the attraction of the materialistic lifestyle is familiar and therefore comforting. Materialism is supported and condoned by our society. We are socialized to believe in it. It is the basis for the American way and the American dream. As you begin to work to change your personal path, you become a pioneer working toward a new dream for all. Once you have made that choice, you will be surprised and pleased to find that there are already many on the path to encourage you and walk with you. In the appendix you will find a list of support groups and organizations that will help to make your journey less perilous and less lonely.

There is no reason that money and the spiritual life cannot walk hand in hand. Any time affluenza becomes a barrier to the flow of money, either in or out, the point of stoppage is fear. As our rich and poor pull farther away from one another in anger, frustration, and fear, so the flow of wealth in our culture becomes slower, more constricted, more "constipated." When we turn to God, we let go of our fear and our need to control. When we begin to look at other people as individuals, as children of God, we become less afraid. Letting go enters every realm of our lives. It is the key to reducing the widening rift between economic classes.

Giving and Receiving

Lifting the veil of fear allows us to see what needs to be done around us, and how we as individuals can help others. With that opening of the heart often comes an opening of the pocketbook. Again, there is no lack of money in this country, only a lack of distribution, and because of money's great transformational quality, it has the potential to bring healing, peace and even prosperity to our ailing society. Steeped in violence, greed, and materialism as it is now, money brings misery and suffering.

Part of the dysfunction of affluenza is the lack of consciousness around the use and distribution of one's money. Part of healing from affluenza is learning a healthy respect for the innate power that money carries. As with any other potentially addictive substance, money will sneak up and grab you in abusive, dangerous ways if you are caught unaware.

Several months ago I sat talking to an elderly friend who remembered the Great Depression clearly. He said that he never saw a homeless, hungry person walk by his home whom his mother didn't invite in and feed. That was the custom, not the exception, throughout their town. Today when we see a person living on the street, we turn our faces away in fear, shame, and disgust, unable to face the truth that "There, but for the grace of God, go I." Changing our belief systems around money and spirituality, wedding the two in a celebration of love, freeing us to share our abundance, would be a great gift to humankind.

Finding a Spiritual Home

On a practical level, I am fully aware of the everyday time constraints with which most of us live. Many affluent people and would-be affluent people are extremely busy either managing their wealth or trying to create it. I believe it is very important for each of us to find a spiritual home, a place where we feel safe and nurtured, surrounded by our family of choice; a place where we can take time from our busy lives to safely nurture our spiritual selves. A spiritual home or community can be a variety of different places: churches, support groups, retreat centers, Twelve Step meetings, wellness centers or centers for spiritual growth. My own spiritual home is Onsite Training and Consulting in Tucson, Arizona, a center for experiential workshops and seminars on various aspects of healing for mental health professionals and others. The people I've met there are my spiritual family of choice. A friend who lived in New York City made her spiritual home at the New York Open Center which offered meditation, therapeutic dance, yoga, tai chi, and all types of body work and other alternative healing classes. She now lives in California and attends a Native American Sweat Lodge Ceremony once a week with a group in Laguna Beach. What all these options have in common is that they are places we can release our anguish and our pain, celebrate our joy, and connect with God on a deeper level. Even fifteen minutes a day spent in some sort of spiritual practice such as prayer or meditation is helpful, but I think it is important that we set aside larger blocks of time that are solely dedicated to our healing and spiritual growth.

As my clientele have increased in number, I have experienced an increasing desire and demand to create a place where we can gather to do more intimate, person-to-person work. Although I present my seminars and workshops in many parts of the country, they are short samples of what a more lengthy healing process has to offer. I am currently working to create a spiritual sanctuary for people with wealth- and money-related problems. It is a process that will be helped considerably by my financial resources, and I am grateful for that.

It is a far easier task to tell you why money doesn't pave the path to happiness than to tell you what does. For each of us, that mysterious journey to find our hearts is an arduous one. We live in a culture of the external and the intellect where people have lost the ability to listen intuitively to the language of the heart. It takes patience and persistence to turn our focus from the outer world to our inner world. To accomplish it, we must often unlearn nearly everything we've been taught about God and religion and begin to quilt together bits and pieces of what truly offers us a sense of peace and joy.

It is the gift of grace that carries us beyond the boundaries of ourselves. By letting go of who we are, we paradoxically become all that God meant us to be. When we start to trust in a power greater than ourselves, we are gently and surely led to trust who we are. We begin to have faith that our experiences and abilities are truly gifts from God.

On the spiritual path that I now travel, whatever I receive along that path that can enhance those whose lives I touch becomes a service to them, myself, and God. I have come to know that what I thought was normal as a child was *not* normal, nor is it what I want in my life now.

As you begin or continue on your personal spiritual quest, gather your tools around you and look forward with courage and hope. If you don't see or feel results immediately, don't despair. Genuine change does not happen overnight. Life, growing up, and recovery from affluenza is about learning how to tolerate frustration and delay gratification. Healing is a process. There is no *there*. We continue to grow and change until the day we die. What makes the spiritual path so beautiful and so desirable is that it transforms aging into a wonderful gift. Each day becomes another step along a path that becomes more radiant and beautiful. The face of our own God becomes clearer and clearer, and we begin to understand with an unshakable certainty that we are not alone and never will be. God bless you and keep you as you embark on this most personal and glorious of journeys.

NOTES

1. P. Ediden, "Drowning in Wealth," *Psychology Today*, April 1989, 35.
2. Philip Slater, *Wealth Addiction* (New York: E. P. Dutton, 1980), 50.
3. Joseph K. Selvaggio, "Many Policies Enrich Wealthy at Expense of Society's Poorest," *Star Tribune*, 18 April 1996, A25.

4. Marianne Williamson, *Sacred Self Workshop* (New York: Sound Horizons Audio-Video, 1994), audiotape.

5. Marianne Williamson, *A Return to Love* (New York: HarperCollins, 1992), 47.

6. George M. Lamsa, trans., *Holy Bible from the Ancient Eastern Text* (Nashville: Holman Bible Publishers, 1957), iii–xii, xvi.

APPENDIX

The Affluenza Questionnaire

TO RECEIVE THE MAXIMUM BENEFIT FROM THIS BOOK, I would highly recommend that you ask yourself these questions. Your answers will be illuminating and healing. Be honest with yourself and as you continue reading gently probe and question your own prejudice and bias toward the wealthy. If you are rich yourself, use this opportunity to examine the level of satisfaction in your life, how your money enhances or detracts. Decide whether the way in which you give of yourself, financially and emotionally, is helping those you love and the world around you. Be gentle with yourself. There is always room and time for change. Do not chastise yourself for things you didn't know. Do not deny that you didn't know them. Acknowledge and feel your emotions. Be grateful that they are there to help you change.

How old are you? Do you have any brothers and sister? What are their ages?

Are you single? Married? Divorced? In a relationship with a significant other?

How many significant relationships have you had in your life? Describe them.

Do you have children? Tell me about them. Who was the Family Founder, the person who made the original fortune? What was your relationship to this person?

How would you describe yourself to yourself?

How do you define affluence?

Do you consider yourself affluent?

Were you raised in an affluent home?

When did you become aware that your family was rich?

How did that awareness affect you as a child?

Do you consider your childhood happy or unhappy and in what specific areas?

How many friends did you have as a child of ten and was that "enough"?

How did your family's affluence affect your upbringing?

Were there servants or other staff in your home?

    If so, how many and what was your relationship to them?

How many true friends do you have now and how do you define friendship?

How has money affected your relationship with others?

Do you find it difficult to trust others?

If yours is inherited wealth, how did that affect your choice of careers?

Have you ever wondered if you could have made it on your own without the money?

    If so, how does this affect your self-esteem?

Do you ever feel that your accomplishments are discounted or not taken seriously?

If so, how does that make you feel and what do you do about it?

If you made it on your own, have you seen a change in your relationships with others?

When people discover your affluence, does it change how they relate to you?

There seems to be a great deal of mystery and secrecy around the subject of money. If you agree, why do you think that's so?

My net worth is about four million dollars. How do you feel about telling me yours? Pay particular attention to the feelings that come up for you as you think about this.

Do you feel guilt? Pride? Fear? Shame? Anger? Nervousness? Any other feelings?

Why do you think you feel that way?

Some people say that money is power and control. If so, how has that aspect of money affected your life?

Have you kept the family name? Why or why not?

In general, do you think your money has been an asset or a liability?

Do you have any other feelings or opinions about the effects of affluence on you or your family?

*   *   *   *

When asking for an interview, it was difficult to ascertain an individual's level of affluence. Common courtesy and respect for their inherent mistrust of others' motives kept me from first asking their net worth. Therefore, I was forced to base my request for an interview on their perceived wealth. In an effort to build trust during the actual interview, I first divulged my net worth and then asked theirs. One person fell substantially under my "qualifying" amount, two refused to answer, and the rest were definitely affluent. Perceived affluence is often based on a person's name or reputation; therefore they are treated as though they have money and the effects upon their psyches are similar. The two subjects who refused to answer reinforced my hypothesis that affluent people are often hesitant or unwilling to discuss their money, particularly the ultimate "intimate" question of their net worth. Although they refused to answer that one question, these same two people were more than ready to share highly personal details about their intimate, family relationships.

I find it interesting and highly revealing that a simple sum of figures takes on such a personal, mysterious, and potentially vulnerable aura that people are afraid to divulge the exact amount. It is as though by revealing this figure, we have somehow defined and exposed ourselves in the most intimate way possible. We fear that upon divulging just how rich we are, we will immediately be judged and categorized. We know that everything we do will be viewed against that backdrop of affluence. This reluctance to divulge our net worth, more than any other characteristic of the wealthy, illustrates the powerful role that money plays in our lives.

I hope this questionnaire will help you and those you choose to share it with to become more aware of your feelings about money. If you have answered the questions honestly, I believe that it will aid you on your journey of recovery from affluenza.

RESOURCES*

The Impact Project's mission is to help people with financial abundance (inherited or earned) realize their life goals and engage their money, talents, and love in building a more just and joyful world. The Impact Project is a member-supported nonprofit organization. See their web site: http://www.efn.org/~impact/

Anne Slepian and Christopher Mogil
21 Linwood St., Arlington MA 02174
617-648-0776, mtmnews@aol.com

Allen Hancock and Tom Berg
2244 Alder St., Eugene OR 97405
541-343-2420, impact@efn.org

For the unabridged (60-page) edition of *Taking Charge of Our Money, Our Values, and Our Lives,* send $24 ppd. to the Impact Project, 2244 Alder St., Eugene, OR 97405.

Publications

TECHNICAL

Brill, Jack A. and Reder, Alan. *Investing from the Heart: The Guide to Socially Responsible Investments and Money Management.* New York: Crown Publishers, 1992. A comprehensive guide, accessible for beginners, presenting an overview of ethical money management and providing detailed analysis of hundreds of specific stocks, bonds, mutual funds, and limited partnerships.

Dominguez, Joe and Robin, Vicki. *Your Money or Your Life: Transforming Your Relationship with Money and Achieving Financial Independence.* New York: Viking, 1992. Guides reader to conscious financial independence and a sustainable lifestyle.

Nolo Press: This publisher of frequently updated self-help law books offers dozens of excellent, inexpensive reference manuals on such topics as: *Plan Your Estate, A Legal Guide for Lesbian and Gay Couples, Divorce and Money, Make Your Own Living Trust.* Contact them for a catalog: 800-992-6656.

Stone, Deanne and Block, Barbara. *Choosing and Managing Financial Professionals.* Booklet guiding the inexperienced investor in the selection of a good financial advisor. Produces by Resourceful Women, 3543 18th Street, #9, San Francisco, CA 94110. Available for $12 ppd.

PERSONAL

Barbanel, Linda. *Piggy Bank to Credit Card.* New York: Crown Publishers, 1993. A practical guide to teaching your children financial skills; organized by different age groups.

Blouin, Barbara; Gibson, Katherine; Kiersted, Margaret. *The Legacy of Inherited Wealth: Interviews with Heirs.* Blacksburg, VA: The Inheritance Project, 1994. Explores the experience of inheriting wealth. Available from the Inheritance Project, 3291 Deer Run Road, Blacksburg, VA 94060.

The Impact Project. *More than Money.* Quarterly journal written by and for people with inherited money and earned financial surplus. "The publication explores how money is linked to virtually every other aspect of our lives—from how we get along in our closest relationships, to how we feel about work, to how we define and pursue our purpose in life." Each issue is peppered with personal stories, practical ideas and humor. Issues include: Money and Spirit; Money and Power, Money and Children. Basic membership is $35/year (for individuals). *More than Money,* 2244 Alder Street, Eugene, OR 97405; 541-343-2420.

Mellan, Olivia. *Money Harmony: Resolving Money Conflicts in Your Life and Relationships.* New York: Walker, 1994. Excellent resource on how to better understand challenging money dynamics in relationships and also how to make them work better.

Mogil, Christopher and Slepian, Anne. *We Gave Away a Fortune.* Philadelphia: New Society Publishers, 1993. Profiles the stories of sixteen people who devoted themselves and much of their wealth to help make a better world. Highlights common issues, such as what's our fair share, personal security, making an impact with giving. Includes a resource list and exercises. Available for $18 ppd. from Impact Project, 2244 Alder Street, Eugene, OR 97405.

SPIRITUAL PERSPECTIVES

Breton, Denise and Largent, Christopher. *The Soul of Economies: Spiritual Evaluation Goes to the Marketplace.* Washington, D.C.: Idea House, 1991. A spiritual and philosophical perspective on economics that challenge old assumptions about our systems and show how they *can* be changed in such a way that we can prosper without greed.

Needleman, Jacob. *Money and the Meaning of Life.* New York: Doubleday, 1991. A philosophical and historical exploration of the relationship between money and the search for spiritual understanding.

Sojourners. "Who Is My Neighbor?: Economics as if Value Matter." A study guide for Christians to make sense of personal economic choices as well as global economics. Includes concrete models for contributing to a new economy and a resource section for further study. Available for $10 from Sojourners, Community, 2401 15th Street NW, Washington, DC 20009, 800-714-7474.

Waldman, Mark. *The Way of Real Wealth.* Center City, MN: Hazelden, 1993. A guide to personal and spiritual growth through exploring how we relate to money. Chock full of stories and useful exercises.

SOCIO-POLITICAL PERSPECTIVES

Brandt, Barbara. *Whole Life Economics: Revaluing Daily Life.* Philadelphia: New Society Publishers, 1995. A practical guide suggesting how to build a healthy economic system drawing from the grassroots economy hidden within the sick dominant economy.

Durning, Alan. *How Much Is Enough?* New York: Norton & Co., 1992. Worldwatch Institute researcher details warnings for the wealthiest fifth of humanity to quickly move away from current consumption to a level of sufficiency, for the sake of a sustainable planet.

Hawkin, Paul. *The Ecology of Commerce: A Declaration of Sustainability.* New York: Harper Collins, 1993. A proposal for how to radically reconceptualize the structure of the economy to support a sustainable planet.

Pizzigati, Sam. *The Maximum Wage.* NY: Apex Press, 1992. A labor journalist makes a case for drastically new federal income tax structures that would limit incomes of the super rich, give tax breaks to everyone else, and revitalize America. Engagingly written.

Organizations

FINANCIAL LITERACY

Haymarket People's Fund: A social change foundation that provides workshops and conferences for people with inherited wealth. Programs cover the personal, technical, political, and funding aspects of taking charge of inherited money. Contact: HPF, 42 Seaverns, Jamaica Plains, MA 02130, 617-522-7676.

Heirs: Provides a forum for beneficiaries of trusts who are discontented with the terms of their trusts. Organizing legislatively for trust reform. Membership includes newsletter. Contact: Heirs, PO Box 292, Villanova, PA 19085; 610-527-6260.

Resourceful Women: Offers an impressive array of classes, support groups, and conferences for women who have $25,000 (or more) of inherited or earned money, to provide personal support, technical assistance, and an empowerment perspective. RW is coordinating a national women's donor network, and a leadership training institute. Contact: RW, Presidio Blvd. 1016, PO Box 29423, San Francisco, CA 94129; 415-561-6520.

Women's Funds: A couple of local Women's Funds offer conferences for women of varying financial means to increase their financial literacy, including workshops on topics like financial planning, investing, funding, and women's economic development. Contact: The Boston Women's Fund, 376 Boylston Street, Boston, MA 02116, 617-375-0035; the Maine Women's Fund, Box 5135, Portland, ME 04101; 207-865-1004.

INVESTING AND SOCIALLY RESPONSIBLE BUSINESS

Businesses for Social Responsibility: An alliance of over 800 businesses that defines and promotes responsible business practices that benefit the community, the economy, and the environment. Publishes a membership newsletter and annual national conference. Contact: BSR, 1030 15th Street NW, Suite 1010, Washington, DC 20005; 202-842-5400.

Coop America: A socially responsible marketplace for consumer goods and services, bringing together socially conscious consumers and businesses. They offer a *National Green Pages* business directory available to members along with a quarterly magazine on building economic alternatives. Membership is $25/year. Contact: CA, 1612 K Street NW, #600, Washington, DC 20006; 202-872-5307.

Investors' Circle: A network of accredited investors committing venture capital to socially responsible companies, sharing ideas, contacts, resources, and due diligence. There are two membership conferences annually as well as regional meetings. Contact: IC, 2400 E. Main Street, Suite 103, St. Charles, IL 60174; 708-876-1101.

Mutual Funds: In the last few years there has been a rapidly growing number of socially screened mutual funds. Several sources offer reports that give you a quick overview of their financial (and social) performance, list fees, and provide contact information. (The beginning investor should please note that this information does not replace the professional services of a financial planner or investment manager.) Contact: The Social Investment Forum, 202-872-5319; *The Green Money Journal,* 509-328-1741, and *Investing for a Better World,* 617-423-6655.

National Association of Community Development Loan Funds: A growing national network of loan funds which lend money to low-income community groups at below-market interest rates. Investors can find out about local funds through the Directory, available for $10. Contact: NACDLF, 924 Cherry Street, 2nd Floor, Philadelphia, PA 19107; 215-923-4754.

The Social Investment Forum: A professional association of socially responsible financial professionals and institutions. Membership is $135/year. Their directory will be available for $6 in Coop America's *Financial Planning Handbook* forthcoming in December 1996. Contact: SIF, 1612 K. Street NW, #600, Washington, DC, 20006; 202-872-5319.

EDUCATION

Centers for Popular Economic Education: Institutes educating the public about traditional and alternative economics through workshops and literature. Contact: Center for Ethics and Economic Policy, 2512 9th Street, #3, Berkeley, CA 94710; 510-549-9931 & Center for Popular Economics, Box 785, Amherst, MA 01004; 413-545-0743.

Ministry of Money: A ministry for people to deepen their faith and to explore their relationship to money from biblical, psychological, and sociological perspectives. M-M publishes a newsletter, holds weekend workshops, and leads soul-opening trips to Third World countries. Contact: M-M, 2 Professional Drive, Suite 220, Gaithersburg, MD 20879; 301-670-9606.

United for a Fair Economy: An organization educating the public about the concentration of wealth and its link to current economic, social, and political problems in the U.S. Offers an amusing and biting newsletter: "Too Much." Contact: UFE, 37 Temple Place, 3rd Floor, Boston, MA 02111; 617-423-2148.

Women's Perspective: A network of women exploring how our attitudes and beliefs about money affect our self-image, relationships, work, and the health of our planet. Open to women of all faith traditions and varied financial means. WP holds workshops. Contact: Rosemary Williams, WP, 115 Puritan Rd., Fairfield, CT 06430; 203-255-2961.

SERVICES SUPPORTING STRATEGIC PHILANTHROPY

Common Counsel Foundation: A consortium of family foundations and individual donors committed to funding economic, environment, and social justice initiatives. Currently seeking new grantmakers to take advantage of their grants evaluation and administration services. Contact: CCF, 2530 San Pablo Ave., Suite B, Berkeley, CA 94702; 510-644-1904.

National Network of Grantmakers: A network including staff and board members of progressive philanthropic organizations and individual donors to social change. NNG holds an annual 3-day conference on social change grantmaking and is developing a national database of social change projects that will be available to grantmakers. Contact: NNG, 1717 Kettner Blvd., Suite 100, San Diego, CA 92101; 619-231-1348.

The Philanthropic Initiative: Provides consulting to corporate, family, and other funders seeking to give more strategically. Offers a newsletter and conferences. Contact: TPI, 77 Franklin Street, Boston, MA 02110; 617-338-2590.

Tides Foundation: Promotes creative philanthropy nationally and internationally in six general areas: land use, economic public policy, environment, international affairs, community affairs, and social justice. TF runs a grantmaking program where individuals and organizations may set up their own donor-advised giving funds. Contact: Tides, Box 29903, San Francisco, CA 94109; 415-561-6400.

Women's Funding Network: A membership organization of about 60 public and private women's foundations, as well as individual donors, promoting the development and growth of women's funds that empower women and girls. Contact: WFN, 1821 University Ave. West, Suite 409 N., St. Paul, MN 55104; 612-641-0742.

PHILANTHROPIC NETWORKS
(OF INDIVIDUALS WITH WEALTH)

A Territory Resource (ATR): A public foundation funding social change activities in the Northwest U.S. The foundation sponsors educational events for donors, and provides a supportive community for those who join as donors and members of the board to evaluate and fund progressive organizations. ATR also provides technical assistance to grantees and supports cultural work related to grassroots organizing. Contact: ATR, 603 Steward Street, Suite 1007, Seattle, WA 98101; 206-624-4081.

Council on Foundations: Provides substantial support services nationally for different sectors of philanthropy, including family foundations, community foundations, regional associations of grantmakers, and philanthropic affinity groups. Along with an annual membership conference, the Council also holds an annual Family Foundation Conference. The Council also publishes guides (such as on how to start a foundation). Contact: COF, 1828 L. Street, NW, #300, Washington, DC 20036; 202-466-6512.

Funding Exchange: A national network of alternative foundations funding progressive grassroots organizations locally and nationally. Community activists have a central role in the grant-making process, and contributions come from a broad spectrum of individual donors. With three national grant-making programs and fourteen local funds operating in twenty-four states, the Funding Exchange network has given over $3 million/year over ten years to grassroots social justice organizations nationwide. FEX holds educational programs for people with inherited wealth, and also offers donor-advised grant-making services. Contact FEX for a list of their local funds, many with programs for people with inherited wealth. Contact: FEX, 666 Broadway, #500, New York, NY 10012; 212-529-5300.

Women Donors Network: Offers peer support, education, and inspiration to women who are giving at least $25,000 annually to social change philanthropy. WDN holds national and regional gatherings. Contact: WDN, Women's Foundation, 3543 18th Street, San Francisco, CA 94110; 415-431-5677.

Experiential Therapists

You can find an accredited experiential therapist by contacting the American Society of Experiential Therapists at 16500 N. Logo del Aero, Tucson, AZ 85739; 520-624-4000, ext. 2048.

For information on training workshops in psychodrama and experiential therapy for groups, write: Tian Dayton, Ph.D., Interlook Inc., 262 Central Park West. No. 4A, New York, NY 10024.

Workshops/Seminars

Affluenza: The Psychology of Money and Wealth
- The myth of the American dream
- Money, codependency, and spirituality
- The psychological profile of the affluent client

The Healthy Wealthy
- How to use your wealth to nurture mind, body, and spirit
- An experiential/educational workshop on accessing the positive aspects of wealth

Children of Affluence
  • How to raise healthy children in an affluent home
  • An experiential workshop on understanding and healing

Adult Children of Dysfunctional Affluent Homes
  • An experiential workshop on understanding and healing
  • How to diagnose and treat the "Silver Spoon" Syndrome

Affluenza and Eating Disorders
  • Money and food

The Losses of Riches
  • Having too much

Medicating Our Misery
  • Affluenza and addiction
  • The power of money

All workshops/seminars can be either experiential, involving vary-ing degrees of client participation, or primarily educational. They vary from one half-day to two days in length. We can also tailor a program to fit your needs.

INDEX

JESSIE O'NEILL is the granddaughter of Charles Erwin Wilson, past president of General Motors and secretary of defense under President Dwight D. Eisenhower. She is a licensed psychotherapist and partner in the Acacia Clinic, Inc., in Milwaukee, Wisconsin, and specializes in the treatment of adult children of dysfunctional homes, codependency, and addiction. She provides individual and group therapy and long distance phone consultations, as well as educational/motivational, spiritual, and therapeautic workshops and seminars.

O'Neill graduated Phi Beta Kappa with a Bachelor of Arts degree in English literature from the University of North Carolina at Chapel Hill and earned a Master's degree in psychology and counseling from Goddard College in Vermont.

She is the mother of two daughters, Rebecca and Maggie, and paints commissioned watercolors of homes.

I am very interested in knowing how money/wealth has affected your life. Please send your stories and comments to

Jessie H. O'Neill, M.A.
8940 Upper River Road
River Hills, WI 53217
Phone/Fax: 414-351-8442
E-mail: JessONeill@aol.com